His Mother

F.C. Butler

Softcover ISBN: 979-8-3492-9271-2
eBook ISBN: 979-8-3492-9272-9
Copyright @ 2025 by F.C. Butler
Publisher: Butler Publishing

This book is the product of visions and lucid dreams put to paper in the wee hours of early early mornings. The author is a trained hypnotist, magician, and seeker of the unknown having studied *NDEs (near death experiences), transcendental meditation, Silva mind control, lucid dreaming, hypnotic regression therapy, Ayahuasca, magic mushrooms (Psilocybin),* and *lysergic acid diethylamide (LSD).* Thru the latter traumatic experience with a … *frantic prayer …* and *plea for help,* … the author **saw Jesus** … and had … **immediate clarity of mind**.

LSD is a potent psychedelic drug that intensifies thoughts, sensory perception, and emotions; it can cause mystical, spiritual, or religious experiences.

It should be noted that the author has … "*never smoked*" … and has … "*never imbibed alcohol*"; … and since that early life traumatic experience, "*never*" experimented with any controversial substance again. He became a firm *believer*, having many lucid prayers answered. Prayers to Jesus are mandatory. That early experience opened the door for future … **answered prayers through Jesus**.

DEDICATIONS

This book is dedicated to all the friends and family members who thought I would never get this book published.

SPECIAL THANKS

Thank you to Sumati Villaman, who put my early hand-written words into a readable computer format.

Thank you to Marilyn Campbell, who helped organize and edit my words from the last 10+ years into a flowing format that made sense.

And, finally, thank you to L. A. Espriux. She helped get my final manuscript into print. She has been invaluable in this whole process, and is an accomplished author who has published several books.

SECTIONS

AWAKENING (PG 7)

KATHIE AND ANA (PG 49)

JONATHAN AND ANA (PG 118)

THERAPY (PG 191)

SECRETS DISCOVERED (PG 220)

COMMUNICATING (PG 282)

EXPLORING CLASSES AND MEMORIES (PG 298)

A SISTER (PG 333)

HAPPY FAMILY (PG 421)

ADVENTURE (PG 444)

CHARACTERS

The Psychic Lady: "Angela"

Anastacia / Ana Romanov: "friend", "girlfriend", "seeker"

Kathie Rothchild: "Ana's best friend & roommate"

Dr. David Danner: "head of Superior General Hospital"

Jonathan Masters: "intern", "boyfriend"

Dr. Franz Anton Mesmer: "mesmerist", "therapist", "counselor", "hypnotist", "father"

Mathew Masterson: "Uncle to Anastacia", "benefactor"

Bill Masters: "Dad to Jonathan"

Dr. Samuel J. Phenom: "psychologist", "BELIEVER"

And others: Anastasia, Tatiana, Maria, and several nurses and doctors

IT IS LEFT TO THE ..."DISCRETION" ... OF THE READER TO DETERMINE IF THIS IS A STORY OF FANTASY OR THE FORETELLING OF POSSIBLE FUTURE EVENTS AS PROPHESIED IN THE ... BLACK BOOK .....

SECTION ONE

AWAKENING

THE LADY AWAKENS

"Well. Lookee here. Our lady awakens. Sitting up in bed. How are you, Dear?"

"Where am I?"

"You're right here in Superior General Hospital. How are you feeling?"

"Who am I?"

"What did you just say?"

"Who am I? … I know *you* … but … I don't know who I am."

"Well, that's an odd question. So … you're having a hard time remembering."

"I remember *you* … *very well*. … I don't have a problem with that. … I just don't know who I am."

"Well, … I'm not sure I'm the person you should be talking to right now."

"I trust you. … I know you."

"Well, … to tell you the truth, … I don't have the credentials *or* the experience. I am just a *new nurse* here at this hospital."

"Sure you do. … Remember when you saved that choking patient at the Christmas party last year? … And you talked that suicidal boy from jumping? … You have *very* good instincts."

"How do you know all that about me?"

"I just know you….. Let's leave it like that for now."

"Well, … it's a little unnerving that you could know those things. … Have we met before?"

"That's what's confusing. … I know *you*. … Why don't you know *me*?"

"Are you telling me that you don't know who *you* are?"

"That is what's so confusing. … I know all about you. … You're married to a lawyer, … a second marriage. … You have two boys and one girl. … You have a so-called *crush* on one of the doctors here, … which I highly advise you *not* to act on. … As soon as you came into my space, … I was flooded with details. … But, … I have no memories of who *I* am. … I know *you*. … You *must* know me."

"Well, … this is quite . … I feel like I've just entered the twilight zone. … You have me *stupefied*."

"I hope you believe me. … I can give you *more* proof that I *really* know you *and* your sister."

"I know what you're going to say. … She gave the same advice you're giving me. … You have convinced me. … I'll do the right thing. … I'll break it off today. ….. Ok. … I'm going to get the doctor to see you. … Just relax. … Don't get out of bed."

A DOCTOR AND THE LADY (ANGELA)

"Oh. ... Please don't come too close. ... It's too confusing."

"But Dear, ... I need to come close. ... I'm your doctor while you're here at our hospital. ... Nurse, what can you tell me about this sweet lady?"

"Ok. But just one of you. Just one at a time. ... Ok?"

"Doctor. ... Will you follow me to the other side of the room?"

(they move to the other side of the room ...)

"Ok, Dear. Is that better?"

"Yes. Thank you."

(whispering ...)

"Boy, Doctor. You have a weird case on your hands with that one."

"Nurse, you should calm down and just tell me what you know ... before I confront her again."

"She was admitted over three weeks ago in a comatose state."

"Yes, that's what it says in her file. So, ... what happened?"

"She woke up ... and ... has lost her memory of herself."

"What is so mysterious about that?"

"Even though she doesn't know who *she* is, ... she seems to know everybody she comes in contact with. ... At least *she* believes that."

"She probably is suffering from some unknown trauma. We will take good care of her."

"There is *more*, Doctor."

"What concerns you?"

"Doctor, it's best if you observe it for yourself."

"Ok. I'll do the talking and you take notes."

(back to the lady ...)

"Ok. Dear, the nurse has just briefed me; and we would like to get more details from you. Is that ok?"

"No. No. You don't understand. It's too confusing, … and it makes me crazy. … Please. Have the nurse stand over there."

"Can you take notes from over there, Nurse?"

"Yes, Doctor. I'm ready when you are."

"Ok, Dear. Let's begin by telling me what you remember."

"Let's begin by not calling me *dear*. I don't like that. It makes me think that you're condescending."

"Ok. What should I call you then?"

(nurse speaking …)

"Doctor, all the nurses call her *Angela*. What about that?"

"Well, what do you think? … Is it ok if we call you *Angela* until we find out who you *really* are?"

"Yes. Ok. … But can you explain why you don't know me? … I know *you*. … I know all about you. The closer you get, the more I know."

"Well, that's very interesting, … BUT … hard to *believe*."

"Well, Doctor, … you're new here. You recently married. Your new wife has three children by a previous marriage. You met her in Italy while on vacation. Her name is Stella. You are going into private practice in Michigan. … Should I go on, Doctor?"

"No, no. That is impressive. I think we will postpone the rest of our visit until another day. I think your new name is appropriate. Enjoy the rest of your day, Angela."

(whispering …)

"Well, Doctor, did I tell you or not?"

"Yes, yes. *That* is quite the experience. She has me in awe. I am going to ask Dr. Danner to assign someone more capable than myself. … Thank you, Nurse."

DOCTOR ENCOUNTER (LITTLE SUSAN)

(A doctor in the Pediatric Cancer Unit at Superior General Hospital with a mother and her young daughter)

"Thanks for seeing me, Dr. Tradough. I have some questions to ask you, but first I would like to thank you for the excellent care you have been giving our little Susan."

"Thank you for that compliment. We try to do the best we can with the challenging circumstances we are up against."

"Well, Doctor, let me get right to the point. What is the prognosis for my Susan?"

"Well, ... the statistics show that ….."

"Please. Please. None of that. Please just tell me the truth as *you* see it, Doctor."

"Your daughter has been with us for some time now, and she has endured some very intense side effects from the chemo. She has endured some real torture, in my opinion. The question to be asked is *when is enough, enough*?"

"Stop. Stop! Doctor, stop. My husband says the same thing. I know where this is going. You just don't understand. She is my life. She is wonderful. She is the nicest and best human being God ever made. Why is God punishing her? … Why is God punishing me? … Take me instead! Please. Just take me. Help. Help me, … please!"

"Please just calm down. Please. You say she talks in her sleep? Do you remember what she says?"

"She seems to be talking to some lady … about how nice everything is. Susan certainly enjoys her naps! That's when she says she can talk with the lady, and that seems to make her very happy."

(Later, little Susan's mother is talking to one of the nurses …)

"Nurse Wilson. Nurse Wilson, can I bother you for a minute?"

"Honey, you're no bother. You and little Susan are special to all of us here at the hospital."

"I just want to personally thank you for the special attention you give to my Susan."

"I love your daughter, as all the nurses and staff do. She has suffered some of the worst this disease gives. What can I help you with?"

"I have a question. Can the medication Susan's taking cause hallucinations?"

"Well, I don't know quite how to answer that. You *do* know that we have dramatically upped the dosage, and normally the side effects can be severe. Quite severe. But for some reason she is very, … how can I say it, … upbeat. She seems to want to sleep a lot. She is talking in her sleep, and seems to be having some good dreams."

"Yes, I have also noticed that she is talking in her sleep. I don't believe she ever did that at home. Is that usual with other patients?"

"Not really. Not that I can recall. But I *do* know that when she wakes up, she is always in the greatest of moods."

(Later, after little Susan wakes up…)

"Mommy, Mommy, can we go for a walk?"

"I'm sorry sweetie, you just received your medicine; and you need to rest now."

"But Mommy, I really need to go for a little walk. It's *really* important."

"Susan, honey, there is nothing more important than you getting better."

"But Mommy, there is someone I really need to see."

"Honey, we're in the hospital. There is no one here except nurses and doctors."

"Aren't there other kids getting treatments … like me … to get better?"

"Yes, but we can't go around bothering people. They need their rest. Just like you do."

"But, … the person I need to see *really* wants to see me and touch my hands."

"How did you come up with that? Has someone been bothering you? You need to explain to me about what you just said."

"I knew you wouldn't understand, Mommy. She is very nice. She is special. And she's in all my dreams."

"Oh. So this is a dream. A *dream lady*?"

"This is more than a dream lady. She is here at the hospital."

"Susan, the medicine you're taking could make you hallucinate and see and hear things that aren't real. I'll ask the doctor. Maybe he can make them stop."

"These are not bad dreams. They are very beautiful and good dreams with fairies and angels. She takes me away from the pain. Don't take her from me. Please, Mommy, don't take her away."

"Honey, don't cry. Thank you for sharing your beautiful dreams with me."

"Mommy, she says I am going to be just fine."

"Well, if she is on our side, she is welcome to be with us. But, for now, you just take a nice nap."

"Ok, Mommy. I hurt only just a little. I know how to find her. I wish we could take you with us on our dream walks."

"Honey, you just go off to sleep now; and you can tell me all about your dreams tomorrow."

"I love you, Mommy."

"I love you more."

"Not possible."

THE REPORT

"There are reports that she roams the halls at night, … visiting sick patients; … and … the next day the patients are miraculously *cured* of their afflictions."

"And, … how did *that* ridiculous rumor start? … Even the nurses on duty report that they have *never* witnessed her outside of her room."

"Well, … it seems only the *patients* claim to have seen her, Dr. Danner."

"There *is* an explanation for this. … How many patients make this claim?"

"Well, … there are six patients that are documented to no longer need the surgery that they had been scheduled for."

"This can no longer go on. … I want these rumors stopped! … I am sure an investigation will prove *all* these allegations to be false."

DOCTORS TALKING ABOUT ANGELA

"Well, Doctor, what do you make of our notorious patient?"

"Fascinating. Just fascinating. … She is progressing very fast. I can't quite grasp how she does what she does, … but … she is very engaging. … It's almost as if she knows in advance what you're up to."

"Well, … my previous reports on her suggest she is an avid reader. … She asks for and receives all kinds of reading material, … from magazines and periodicals to books, … etc."

"Yes. I noticed the stack of books beside her bed. And the curious thing is how she scours over them. … She does it so fast, it's hard to believe she can retain any of it."

"Well, she has been tested on that."

"How so?"

"Just point to any book in that huge pile. … Give her a page number, … and she will recite it to you word for word."

"That sounds like she may possess … savant traits."

"But, that doesn't explain *how* she seems to know *personal* things about the people who come into her space."

"I agree … that there seems to be something *supernatural* going on here."

"Whoa Doctor!! … We don't go there. … I don't subscribe to anything but *scientific* facts, … and I insist that no one in my hospital endorses anything *but* that. Understood?"

"Yes, … Dr. Danner. … Understood."

NURSES TALKING

"How does she do it? ... Do you think she is the real deal? ... Is there really something to this *psychic* stuff?"

"Well, ... I have to admit there certainly is something very strange going on here. She is upending my belief system. There must be a rational explanation for all this."

"Have you heard all the stories going around the hospital? ... All the nurses are going to visit her after their shifts are done. She seems very willing to engage and seems to be giving credible advice."

"But ... are these harmless interactions, or are we impeding her recovery? ... She still has no memory of herself coming through to her; ... but ... when someone else comes into her space, she professes to be flooded with all kinds of information about them. How do you explain that?"

"Well, ... the head honcho, Dr. Danner, is reported to be very upset by all this; and he wants, as he puts it, *this nonsense to be stopped*. ... I understand he is taking all the head doctors for a visit and confrontation and evaluation of the poor lady. That will be interesting."

THE DOCTORS ENCOUNTER THE LADY

"May we come in?"

"I have been advised you would be visiting with me."

"I would like to introduce you to my staff and to myself. ... I am Dr. David Danner, head of this hospital; and I have the honor of leading these distinguished colleagues of mine in any manner that is of benefit to you."

"Yes. ... I know you want to help me, ... or ... it may be more accurate to say you want to investigate all the rumors you no doubt have heard about me."

"I can see you understand the situation quite well."

"Doctors, ... let me tell you quite frankly, ... I really don't know what is going on here. ... It's as if I'm coming out of a fog."

"Can you try to explain to us a little of what you're experiencing?"

"Yes. ... It's quite simple. ... I woke up ... and I don't know who I am, ... BUT ... somehow I know *you*."

"What do you mean, … *you* know *us*?"

"Just like I said, you come into my space, … and … it's as if I know you … and … anybody that I have met so far. … I'm confused. … If I know *you,* all about *you,* … why don't you know *me*?? … Why don't I know *me*? … It's overwhelming."

"I can see your situation is a little upsetting to you. … Can you describe what you're going through?"

"Sir, … you in the back, … can you come to me, please?"

"Sure. I am pleased to meet you. … I'm Dr. Franz Anton Mesmer."

"I know who you are. … Let's stop with the formalities. I am being flooded with information about you."

"Really? … How interesting. … And what are you getting?"

"You have, … shall I say, … a very famous ancestry line."

"Can you elaborate?"

"Your great great grandfather founded the name *Mesmerism* … and … was very controversial in his time, … wasn't he?"

"Well, … I have been assigned to work with you, … and … I can see that it's not going to be boring, … is it?"

"Your grandfather has notoriously haunted you all your life … You have unwillingly inherited his full name, and you have been subjected to somewhat cruel jokes about Mesmerism. … And something about France. … Oh. … Shall I go on?"

"You are very interesting … You make me feel like I am in reverse therapy."

"Dr. Mesmer, I'm also getting some personal ….."

"Let's stop right there. … We won't bother my revered colleagues with any more boorish information. … I have the pleasure of being assigned to some rather extensive sessions with you."

"I like you, Doctor. … I'm being flooded with some very good things about you."

"I very much like you too."

"Well, I can see we're off to a good start here."

"Doctors, … may I make a request of all of you?"

"And what might that be?"

"I would like to shake hands with each of you."

"I'm sure that would be our pleasure."

"It might be a little more like holding hands for a brief moment … Is that ok?"

AN INTERACTION WITH THE LADY

"Excuse me, Ma'am, I don't want to startle you."

"May I advise you that you won't. I have been expecting you."

"That is a strange thing to say. This is random. I am not scheduled to visit you."

"You are here to evaluate my cognitive status. Is that correct?"

"That and many other things. I have been assigned to be of assistance in any way I can as I fit you into my rather busy schedule."

"Well, this should not take too long."

"Well, Ma'am, first may I introduce myself … I am Dr. Phenom."

"Can I ask of you, Dr. *Samuel J.* Phenom, to do something you will find rather awkward? Come closer. Let me hold your hand for a moment."

"Well, I'm afraid I would consider that inappropriate."

"I expected that from you, Dr. Phenom. But if you want to get off to a fruitful beginning, then YOU WILL."

"Alright. … I will reluctantly oblige."

"Now, … just look into my eyes for a moment."

"You're not attempting hypnosis here are you?"

"No. No, Doctor, just bear with me here."

"May I ask what you're attempting to do?"

"To use your terminology, I'm *picking up on you*, … so to speak."

"And may I ask ….."

"You want me to explain to you what is transpiring here?"

"If you are so willing."

"You were one of the top four achievers in the high IQ Mensa society program. You exhibited condescending traits with whoever you considered to be beneath your mental intellectual status at Harvard. And you, sir, are a very very religious man. May I quote Matthew 24:36, '*But of that day and hour no one knows…*' And you are entering a realm you are *not* adequately qualified to explore, and your report would *not* set you in good standing with Dr. David Danner."

"Yes, you are very accurate so far of your assessment of the situation here. The head of Superior General Hospital is a no-nonsense atheist, and he has no qualms expressing his belief; and he expects everyone to adhere to *his* way."

"And how does that sit with you, Dr. Phenom?"

"You are very accurate at your assessment of me. I am a true *believer*. … Why are you interested in my spiritual beliefs? And why do you express that you would *already* know my conclusions to our interactions?"

"As I'm sure, you are aware of my *supposed* unusual talents; and I am picking up on you very appropriately, Doctor. You are of superior intellect in comparison to your peers and your demeanor is condescending. We would not resonate, so to speak."

"Well, that is a very blunt and to the point analysis of our situation here. It has been, shall I say, *very overwhelming*."

"It *has* been very interesting, hasn't it … Dr. Samuel J. Phenom."

NURSES TALKING AGAIN

"How does she do it?"

"Nurse Sally says her reading was very accurate and just couldn't believe how she could know so much about her family. She swears by her."

"I heard about Nurse Beverly coming back from lunch and apologizing to the lady for being late saying some lame excuse, … and the lady saying she will think back on this day … nine months from now. She is having a boy."

"What about that telekinesis thing where she asked the nurse to get her something on the other side of the room, … and nurse Betsie said to wait just a minute. Before she could, … the lady had it on her bed."

"And … what about when you're ready to ask her something, … and … she answers you before you speak."

"I understand there are over twenty or more testimonials on the lady."

"She … is quite the fascinating lady alright."

THE LADY AND DR. MESMER

"So, … Dr. Franz Anton Mesmer, you're following up on me, as you suggested you would when you first visited me with your esteemed colleagues."

"You have a good recollection."

"I remember being fascinated by your famous lineage. Does the date 1734 mean anything to you, Dr. Mesmer?"

"Already you start our first session by fascinating *me*."

"You, Doctor, also share the same birth date. Am I also correct on that?"

"Well, Young Lady, … I see that the gossip that precedes my visit to you was well warranted. You seem to be very well tutored on my lineage."

"Yes, Doctor, … I seem to be picking up on you as we speak."

"I have heard the stories about your unusual *supposed* ability. Do you have an explanation of how this happens?"

"I do not. … I just seem to, … well, … it's like … it's like I have always known you. … When someone comes close, … I feel flooded with all this information. … It's very overwhelming … but I guess I'm coming to terms with it now."

"Interesting. … Very interesting. I may just devote my next book to what transpires in our investigation of your condition."

"Dr. Mesmer, your attempt at humor is refreshing. … I'm comfortable with you."

"Young Lady, we're off to a good start. I look forward to our future sessions together."

"Doctor, thank you for referring to me as a *young* lady."

"Well, … in my opinion you *are* a *young* lady."

"Just so you know, Doctor, … I am a lot, lot *older* than you can ever imagine."

"Young Lady, … I'll stick to my first impression."

AFTER THE VISIT: DOCTORS' BRIEFING

"Well, Gentlemen, what do you make of that meeting with the lady?"

"She asked to shake each of our hands and look straight at her."

"Yes, … that certainly was unusual."

"Did you notice how she closed her eyes and seemed to go off somewhere when she asked to hold our hands?"

"I think that was her way of picking up on us … individually."

"Doctor Mesmer, … I want a full evaluation of what is transpiring here. … Can you work in a daily session with her?"

"No, Dr. Danner, I cannot. … But … may I suggest that your new intern that you are expecting, Jonathon Masters, would be an excellent person to be in charge of your project. … I was very impressed with his credentials."

"That is an excellent recommendation, now that I think of it. … That would be a perfect way to get him started when he arrives here at our hospital."

"And, I would be glad to be in charge of supervising him, Dr. Danner."

"Ok, then, Doctor Mesmer. … We have a good plan here."

DR. JUNA AND DR. MESMER

"Dr. Mesmer, … how are you? … It's been a while. … How have you been?"

"Well, well. … Look who's here. … Dr. Thomas Juna, … I was told you would attend this special meeting. You're looking good. … You've gained a couple of much needed pounds."

"Yes, yes. … It's a good life. … There are too many fine restaurants around here."

"Well, … Thomas, … what is *so urgent* that we all are required to attend this *special* meeting?"

"Well, Franz, … I think we are about to meet the new intern we have been hearing so much about."

"You mean *Bill's boy*?"

"That's the one. … He graduated number one in his class at Harvard. … Just like Dr Danner."

"I remember well the competition that we witnessed. … It was intense."

"It was all in good fun, … *watching them go at it*."

"I think we were *all* in competition back then, Thomas."

"Yes, … but it was Bill and David who stood out. … Always competing to be the best."

"Well, … David Danner won out. … *He* graduated number one."

"If you remember, Bill was *so close*. … You really couldn't tell *who* was the *real* winner."

"That is why Bill's *son* was pushed to the number one of his class."

"We *all* benefited from our fraternity. … We were all so close knit."

"Well, … here we are. … All success stories by *anybody's* standard."

"Well, … you know Bill Masters is the *wealthiest* of us all. … He is the founder of that tech company that keeps making headlines."

"You do know that Bill just paid for the new wing on our prestigious hospital here, Dr. Juna?"

"Well, … he can afford it. … He's listed as one of the top richest men in America. … So, … is that why his *son* is interning here?"

"Possibly. … We're going to meet the young lad in a short while."

"What is his name?"

"His name is Jonathon Masters."

THE MEETUP BETWEEN THE LADY AND DR. DANNER

"So, ... the *head honcho* visits with me on his own. ... I remember *well* your first visit with your colleagues."

"Well, ... yes, ... I *am* the head of the hospital. ... I'll be doing my best to make your stay with us as pleasant as possible."

"I have been anticipating our encounter, ... and hope we can have a fruitful conversation."

"Well, ... I hope my staff hasn't been *too* harsh with what they have to say about my protocols."

"Well, ... frankly, ... since your *new* protocols, ... nobody will give me anything more than *pleasantries*. ... I think you put the *fear of wrath* in them. ... I believe that *those* encounters greatly helped me in my quest to regain my personality. ... I had no idea, at the time, that my talents were not shared by everyone else. ... Apparently, this has branded me as a *psychic* or even worse, ... a *witch*."

"Well, well. ... I see that we're going to get along very well. ... You now have a better understanding of *why* I put my directives in place. ... With a little tutoring and a little role playing, we can have some fun with these *paranormal rumors*. ... Are you up for it?"

"What do you have in mind, ... *Dr. David Danner*?"

"I have brought you eight books, ... all on the art of magic. ... There are tutorials on learning to manifest your so-called *psychic* abilities from A to Z on anything paranormal."

"I get it. ... Once people find out I have studied the art of magic, ... it will dispel their fear of my being a witch."

"Honey, ... you've got the idea. ... I'm assuming you're on board?"

"This should be fun. ... I'll devour them tonight."

ONE WEEK LATER

"Hi Angela. ... Sorry it took so long getting back with you. ... How are you doing with our fun project?"

"Well, ... I'm certainly having *fun* with this project. ... I became so caught up with it that I ordered every book that I could think of on any related subject."

"Like what are you talking about?"

"Well, … like meditation, … Uri Geller's spoon bending, … faith healing, … Stephen Hawking, … David Blaine, … Albert Einstein, … and Isaac Newton. … I feel compelled to devour everything I can. It's like coming out of a dream … or going *into* one. … I have to be careful here. … You know, … that *mumbo jumbo* stuff."

"Well, … I can see that you take your projects seriously. … What's with those bent spoons on your table, Angela?"

"Oh, … that's the *Uri Geller effect*. … I do it a little differently. … Do you want to see something levitate, Dr. Danner?"

"Don't you need some invisible thread? … See. … I have read a *little* about magic too."

"So you have. … But as I said, … I do it a little *differently*."

"I'm not ready for you to challenge my belief system just yet, Angela."

THE SESSIONS

"Well, Dr. Mesmer, … you have experienced a couple sessions with her. Any insights happening here?"

"This is the most *fascinating* case I have ever experienced."

"Well, … that certainly is an *intriguing* way of putting it. Can you elaborate?"

"I can't make up my mind about her. … I truly believe she is *sincere*. … and believes *everything* she says to be *true*."

"What do you mean by *that* statement?"

"Well, … everyone she comes in contact with believes she's *psychic*."

"Why? … Does she give readings to them … like the other *phone psychics* do?"

"No, … not exactly. … She just tells them things that *supposedly* no one knows about. … Personal things."

"Is she accurate?"

"*That* … is part of my assessment."

"How do you go about that, Dr. Mesmer?"

"I have interviewed all the people that I know … who … have had extensive time with her."

"And your *conclusion*?"

"Everyone *believes* she possesses *psychic* abilities. … They say they have witnessed some *amazing* things."

"Like what?"

"I really don't want to talk about that … *until* … I investigate further."

"What are you *investigating*?"

"*Psycho kinesis,* moving things with your mind, … reading people's thoughts, … fortune telling, … the *whole gamut*."

"Well, … you possess a lot of credentials. … You're a famous author, … highly respected psychiatric hypnotherapist, … and have a very famous lineage."

"And I am *very* concerned that my findings … could … adversely affect my *reputation*."

"Yes, … you are *treading on thin ice*, … so to speak."

"All the evidence *seems* to be in her favor."

"Are there *any* discrepancies?"

"Yes. … YES. … I found that she is not *always* correct in what she says."

"Do you have a story to tell here?"

"It's kind of personal, … but … I'll tell you the story."

"I'd like to hear it."

"I had heard the stories about her giving readings to people, and they *seem* to be accurate; … but people tend to hear what they *want* to hear. … So, … I decided to evaluate what she would tell *me* about *myself*. … I asked her to tell me what she could, … about me."

"How did that turn out?"

"First, … I *was* amazed. … She was so accurate. … She knew that I was very embarrassed about being named after my so-called famous grandfather. … She knew that I was very shy, … and she knew some *very personal things* that … I believed nobody could possibly know about."

"Can you give me some personal details, … so … *I* can also evaluate her credibility?"

"Well, … this is going to be a little bit embarrassing for me, … but … I'll try to be as accurate and open as I can."

"I promise this is all confidential."

"Something happened in college that only *I* knew about, … BUT … *she* knew that. … To be sure that she wasn't guessing, … I grilled her; and she started talking about things that I had forgotten or, … to be truthful, … had *suppressed*. … I asked her to give me details … so … I could evaluate how her mind works."

"What happened?"

"It was *amazing*. … It was as if she was reviewing my past."

"Can you give details?"

"She told me … *exactly* … how I thought at that time. As I previously said, I was painfully shy, … BUT, … I was always told how *handsome* I was. … I guess I started to believe it, … and … so … I started to experiment with self-hypnosis; … and … *it worked*. … I talked myself into having the confidence to approach the beauty queen on campus. … We had a torrid affair for about a month. …

Then … she dropped me, … and I never heard from her again. … After *that* disappointment, … the shyness returned; … and I didn't date for a long time. … I met this very dedicated law student, and we married shortly after college. … The lady was pretty accurate up to this point."

"What do you mean, … *up to this point*?"

"Like I said, … she was *uncannily accurate* up to this point."

"Ok. … Where is the kick?"

"In her telling me about myself, … she said … that I have *two beautiful daughters.*"

"I didn't know you have children."

"I don't. … I don't. … *That's* the kicker. … My wife didn't want children. … I got a vasectomy some time after we were married. … Everything *else* was *very* accurate."

"Well, … I can see you have some … *real challenges* here."

"Wish me luck!"

"You are going to need it."

THIS HAS TO STOP

"Listen closely. … I need to put a *stop* to this nonsense. … There is no such thing as the *paranormal*, … and … our reputation is at stake here."

"Have *you* read the reports?"

"Of course I have, … and it's all *nonsense*. … She is probably *delusional*. … After all, … she *was* in a coma."

"The nurses' reports seem to be very credible and competent."

"Well, … *that's* debatable. … Some of these reports read like fiction. … Fortune telling, … teleportation,… mind reading,… etc….. What is this world coming to? … Of *course* I'm agitated. It's *got to stop*! … It *will* stop. … Gather my staff. … I want a meeting."

"Right away, Dr. Danner."

SECTION TWO

KATHIE AND ANA

I WANT TO MEET THAT LADY

(Best friends meet again after four years …)

"I want to meet that lady ….."

(Kathie comes up behind Anastacia …)

"What!! …What did you just say?! … Anastacia Romanov. … Turn around! … Stand up! … And give me a big hug."

"Kathie, … I didn't see you come in. I have been so engrossed listening to those fascinating stories … about the lady. … I want to meet that … *psychic* lady."

"Yes. I heard my hospital staff reading to you classified personal accounts about the lady, and they know that they are in trouble for doing that."

"So, … that's why they all turned away when they saw you come up in back of me."

"They know all about the direct order that Dr. Danner, the head honcho at this prestigious hospital, gave about *not* spreading gossip about the lady."

"So, … are the stories about the lady *true*?"

"Of course not, Ana. Do you actually believe that someone can know all about you just by you going into their space … or tell your fortune … or read your mind … and all the other nonsense they say about her?"

"Well, … there are over twenty stories that your staff read to me while I was waiting for you to get out of your meeting."

"Why do you find that so intriguing?"

"I have my reasons."

"Well, … we have better things to discuss, like … how was your flight over here? … I know how you don't like flying."

"It was terrible, Kathie, … but I have a cute story to tell …"

"I'm listening."

"The plane flew into some major turbulence. … Things went flying. … People were screaming. … And a mother looked over at me and said, 'Look how calm that lady is, just reading her book.' … The little boy said to his mother, 'Look. Her book is upside down. Busted!!'"

"I'm just glad you made it safely here, Ana. … It has been over four long years since we last saw each other. We have a lot of catching up to do. … Let's get out of here and go to our new cafeteria so we can talk and catch up."

"Great idea, Kathie. I'm famished."

"Hey. … Look over there, Ana, … coming through the entrance. I recognize him. I think it's the new intern we have been expecting to arrive at Superior General."

"He's looking our way."

"Just nod at him as we go by. … Did you see the way he was staring at you?"

"Who is he anyway, Kathie?"

"His father donated the funds to build the state of the art trauma wing at our hospital. This was a big deal. Wouldn't you like to meet him?"

"Heck no! He is *too* good looking and probably has women drooling all over him all the time. … I bet his ego is *off the charts*."

"Well, … just look at you, … always wearing those big dark ugly glasses so people can't see how beautiful *you* are."

"It's because people always mistake me for that famous actress. … It's very embarrassing."

"Yes, Ana, it's very hard being one of the *pretty people*, isn't it?"

"I wish you wouldn't kid me about this."

"Well, … we're going to have to come up with a way to cash in on your good looks."

"Let's change the subject, shall we? … I want you to tell me all about that new place. What's it called … *Utopia,* or something like that?"

"It's everything I told you about. … I can't wait for you to see it."

"You have me all excited about it, Kathie."

"Listen. I need you to listen to me. … You wanted to know about that so-called *psychic lady*?"

"I was so caught up in all those intriguing stories your office staff was telling me about the lady."

"Well, … you need to know that you shouldn't go there, Ana."

"Why. Why not? I *really* want to meet with her."

"The head of this hospital, Dr David Danner, is very concerned about the reputation of his hospital, … and he has put out a memo … *No more gossip about the lady!* Dr. Danner is a no-nonsense kind of man; and he is *totally,* and I mean TOTALLY, against what is transpiring with that so-called *psychic* lady. … Why is it you want to meet with her, Ana?"

"Have you read the reports, Kathie? There are over twenty statements as to her credibility."

"You're not listening! You need to listen to me! Dr. Danner is intent on debunking her. Why are you risking everything!?"

"Because, … she knows who my … *biological* … father is!"

ANASTACIA'S DIARY

Dear Diary .....

It's my decision, isn't it? ... After all, I have a right to know who my biological father is ... don't I? ... Kathie is my best friend ... no ... my sister ... almost. After all, we grew up together. ... I hope she understands my need to know. ... He was a great Dad to both of us. ... He was just NOT my biological father. ... She will understand. ... I hope.

JONATHAN MASTERS MEETS DR. DAVID DANNER

"Please, may I ask directions to Dr. David Danner's office?"

"Oh yes. Continue down this hall, and you'll find his office directly behind the reception area."

(*at the reception area ... *)

"I believe Dr. Danner is expecting me. I am Jonathan Masters."

"Yes, you're right on time. Dr. Danner is expecting you. Go right in."

"There you are. Right on time. Please sit down …. Well, well, my boy. We finally meet and I feel as if I know you. I was, as you know, best friends with your father in our Harvard days."

"Yes, Dr. Danner, I've heard all about you all my life. My father thinks so highly of you."

"Well, we were best friends and great competitors, as well."
"My understanding is that you graduated number one in your class at Harvard, barely beating out my father."

"Yes, it was rewarding; and great friends we are. We both were so driven."

"Boy, haven't I ever known *that* all my life. I heard those fantastic stories, Dr. Danner."

"Well, they're only half true. We both tend to embellish a little."

"Well, they certainly inspired me to follow in your footsteps."

"Your father and I maybe could have been overachievers in our competition."

"Without that competition, I probably wouldn't have achieved what I have, Dr. Danner. And I am very aware of your deep friendship. That's why I'm here at Superior General Hospital."

"We're so glad to have you intern here. It's a great honor to have a number one Harvard graduate on our team."

"Yes, it was very important that I achieve the number one status that eluded my dad."

"Well, look at what your father has accomplished in the business world."

"I'm as proud of Dad as he is of me. I couldn't have achieved what I did without his drive and inspiration."

"We're proud that you chose to intern here at our hospital. And we're so looking forward to the completion of our new wing that your father has so generously funded. It will be named after your family, Jonathan."

"Dad was so happy he could be the one to do it, and he asked me to be on the lookout for anything else you could be wanting or needing."

"Yes, he has advised me that we have an open check; and we are so very grateful for his generosity. Thanks to your family, we will have the most advanced medical equipment in the country. And have you had a chance to look around at all the renovations that are taking place at our hospital thanks to your family's generous donations?"

"Well, I arrived a little early and your guard suggested I go to your new cafeteria; and, if I hurried, I could get a glimpse of some famous actress that was dining there."

"I heard about that too … but … as it turns out, she is just a newly arrived friend of our Office Administrator, Kathie Rothchild."

"Well, I went to the cafeteria and arrived just in time to see the most attractive lady I've ever laid eyes on."

"Yes, people around here like to gossip; and sooner or later, I hear everything. And I don't approve of gossip. Jonathan, you couldn't have arrived at a better time here at Superior General Hospital. In just the last few weeks, we've had major breakthroughs in what were once considered as incurable cases. We've had a record number of remissions and complete healings."

"I overheard one of your nurses being ecstatic over the unexpected and, as she called it, *miraculous recovery* of that little girl named Susan."

"I don't believe in miracles! Just good research breakthroughs and a dedicated staff are the answer for our remissions."

"Well … I certainly want to be a part of the Superior General Hospital's success story."

"Like I said, Jonathan, you couldn't have arrived at a better time."

JONATHAN (THE FIRST ENCOUNTER)

As I entered the room, … she … was sitting upright, … erect in her bed, … as if anticipating my coming.

Our eyes met, … and … the strangest feeling overwhelmed me. … She put her finger to her lips in a gesture I interpreted to mean … not to talk. … She … motioned for me to come sit beside her on the bed, … and … again gestured … not to talk. … I complied with her wishes … and … sat on the edge of the bed.

As I looked at her face, … her eyes fixed on mine. … We locked into a pleasant stare. … She held out her hand in a gesture to beckon mine. … As our hands grasped gently, … I could feel tears flooding my eyes … in … tandem with this stranger's eyes.

A pleasantness overwhelmed my being … as … I slowly digested that this being was no stranger to my soul. … The essence of me was revisiting … something … I could not explain.

CURRENT EVENTS

"Angela, I have brought you your daily newspaper, as you requested."

"Thank you very much, Jonathan. ... There are so many stories that I read about."

"Well, ... I find it hard to digest all the *bad* things that are happening in our world, Angela."

"Yes, ... I see how it *can* be disturbing the way this world is headed."

"Why are ... *YOU* ... so passionate about keeping up with current events, Angela?"

"Well, ... *someone* needs to be concerned. ... That's a reasonable assumption. ... Don't you agree, Jonathan?"

"We should *all* wake up to what's happening. ... These are DANGEROUS times. ... Wars, ... nuclear threats, ... Artificial Intelligence. ... It's scary."

"Yes, ... I agree. ... Someone *should* come and give a *stern warning*."

"I'm with you on that, Angela. ... Maybe ... we should *PRAY* ... that someone does."

"That is the *best advice* I have *ever* heard."

"I have my fingers crossed."

"It will take a little bit *more* than that, ... but ... you *are* on the right track."

"Would you like to be here for *that* event ... when some powerful figure gives a *stern* warning to the world?"

"Yes, ... I would very much like to attend *that* event. ... Very, very much."

"I think a prominent figure should take center stage, Angela, ... and tell it like it is. ... Then we'll *HOPE* ... and ... *PRAY* ... that people heed the warnings."

"My advice is to forget the first thing, ... *HOPE* ... and concentrate on the *LAST* word ... *PRAY*."

"And for me, Angela, ... I seem *compelled* to keep up with current events."

"Yes, Jonathan, ... everybody has to find their calling."

IT'S NICE TO SEE YOU

"Dr. Mesmer, … it's nice to see you."

"And Angela, … you're looking rather *perky and alert* this fine morning."

"I *feel* perky, … as you say. … I enjoy your slang."

"How have you been feeling, … in general?"

"Fine, … just fine. … How is your evaluation about me coming?"

"Well, Angela, … your blood work is fine. … You've gained some weight, and that's good. … Let's talk about your *mental* state of being."

"Ok. … What do you want to know? … Oh. … I *already* know that."

"Are you … *already* … reading my mind?"

"Ha. Ha. … That's funny. … You *know* you don't believe in that … *nonsense*, … as Dr. Danner puts it."

"Well, … you certainly know where *we're* coming from."

"I do. … I *do* know that."

"Can you give me an explanation for what has transpired here?"

"Ok. Ok. … I can *try* to explain … in a way you can accept. … *MAYBE.*"

"I'm listening."

"Well, … I am aware that I *must* have caused quite the concern."

"That's absolutely correct."

"When I first arrived, … I wasn't fully there. … I had not received my *full* mental state. … I was in a state of confusion."

"What do you mean by … not … fully arriving?"

"You're not ready … for … *that* answer, Doctor."

"Ok. … I'll accept that. … Please continue."

"I know you have to submit your findings to Dr. Danner."

"No. … No, not exactly, … if you want to tell me something *in private.*"

"Believe me, Doctor, … you're *not* ready."

"I wish you would try."

"Well, … you know I am working with Jonathan. … We're on a first name basis."

"Yes. … I believe you know … that … Jonathan and I have agreed to collaborate on your case."

"I am very aware of that. … You two are *very* different."

"How do you mean that?"

"You have very different *belief* systems, … don't you?"

"Yes, … I guess that could be interpreted as correct."

"I have spent many hours … with Jonathan, … and … he has been very *beneficial* in my development."

"How do you explain all the *rumors*?"

"I'll try in basic layman's terms. … When I first became conscious, … I *believed* I was acting normal. … In other words, … I thought that *everybody* … could do what I could do."

"The rumors stated that you exhibited all sorts of *psychic* behavior."

"Yes, ... but I found a way to be accepted as *normal*."

"I'm listening."

"You're aware that ... I am an *avid reader*."

"Yes, ... I have been told that."

"Well, ... we let it be known that I have an interest in *magic*."

"Ok."

"And, ... that I had devoured *every* ... *how to* ... *magic book* I could get my hands on. ... And ... that's *true*. ... *I really did*."

"So, ... that's your explanation?"

"Yes. ... And ... in your report you should state that ... I ... am *very good* at it.... *Because I am*."

"Well, well. ... You *have* come up with a *very* plausible explanation, ... haven't you?"

"What do you think?"

"Let's leave *that* for further debate."

"I agree, Doctor. … I agree."

JONATHAN AND DR. MESMER

"I don't think I am ready yet, Doctor, to divulge my findings with *anyone*."

"That's the only way this can work. You have to trust me, Jonathan."

"Doctor Mesmer, I greatly respect you; and I don't want you to lose respect for me."

"I respect that you have come to me in the first place."

"I would rather you find out for yourself, Doctor. … You're assigned to investigate the lady, aren't you?"

"Yes. I have already had a brief encounter with her when Dr. Danner had all of us as a group visit her and later a few visits by myself."

"So, … what was your first impression?"

"Well, Jonathan, she is supposedly able to know all about you when you enter her space."

"What happened?"

"We determined she was *not* credible. She gave us stories that were *not* factual."

"So, … you are assigned, as I am, to follow up on the lady, … right Dr. Mesmer?"

"Are you asking if there could be a conflict of interest?"

"Yes, … I guess that *is* the question."

"I would rather think of this as a collaboration. We can agree to share our findings and experiences."

"We both know how Dr. Danner sees this. He is a no-nonsense sort of guy and fully expects the results to be of his liking."

"Yes, … that puts everything in perspective."

"So, … how to handle this, Doctor."

"Ethically, … the truth … is the truth."

"I like that answer. Now I am fully on board, … on one condition."

"What is that, Jonathan?"

"That our collaboration will remain confidential. You know that Dr. Danner is going to want reports."

"I will tell him, … remind him, … that I have to honor privacy; and my ethical responsibility is foremost. Don't worry. I guarantee our privacy."

"If I can be assured and promised by you, … I'll take you at your word."

"Jonathan, you have my word."

"Ok. Ok. … Where do we begin?"

"You talk, Jonathan. I listen."

"First, … this is beyond difficult for me. … I am always putting myself in your shoes and deciphering what … you … would think."

"I understand, Jonathan, … and I am committed to be open, … impartial, and non-judgmental in all we do here."

"Well then, … here goes."

"I'm listening … closely."

"This is going to be harder than I thought it would be, Dr. Mesmer."

"I hear you."

"Ok. … First, … we have advanced."

"You and the lady?"

"Yes."

"Explain."

"We, … communicate … without speaking."

"Ok, ok."

"Do you know … what … I am saying?"

"Yes, Jonathan. You communicate *telepathically*."

"You … do understand this. Sort of."

"Yes. Please continue."

"At our frequent sessions, … I felt as if I knew her, … as if … I have *always* known her. I don't know any other way to explain this, Dr. Mesmer, … and … I can imagine how this comes across."

"Thank you, Jonathan, for explaining as you have. … And I agree, … this could be perceived as some sort of *hallucination*. I will be *alert* ... and *aware* ... when it's *my* next encounter with the special lady. ... And ... we could use a second opinion."

JONATHAN AND THE SECOND OPINION DOCTOR

"And so, ... how is my good friend Dr. Mesmer doing these days?"

"He is doing fine ... and sends his regards."

"I received his message that he wanted you to consult with me, Jonathan."

"Yes. ... He suggested that you could provide me with answers or knowledge about what I'm dealing with"

"Well, ... that remains to be seen. ... What knowledge are you seeking?"

"To get right to the point, ... I have been confronted with circumstances that challenge my belief system."

"That ... is a very interesting way of presenting your plight."

"And, ... as I understand it, ... you are involved in investigating fringe science."

"Yes, Jonathan, I have the dubious reputation of being … the … foremost *quack* doctor in town."

"I can see that you are … not … concerned about that."

"You are correct about that, my boy. … And you, sir, have a reputation as being our newest and brightest hope for the future."

"So, … do you know about me, Doctor?"

"I also have done my research … and am very impressed with your accolades. … Number one in your class at Harvard … and so on."

"Do you know Dr. Danner?"

"Yes. … I am also a Harvard graduate, only much farther down the line; … but … I managed to secure my place in the Mensa program."

"Oh, … so you know about that."

"Yes, Jonathan, … I have been involved in everything … but … the *society* thing."

"So, … you *do* know about the *secret society thing*?"

"I know that is one thing … I … am not allowed to talk about."

"I respect that, Doctor."

"Thank you. … I don't need to invoke trouble, … but … I'll try to be available for any other subject you wish to discuss."

"I greatly appreciate your candor. … Can I ask, … since you seem to come from the Harvard era that I'm investigating, … do you know my father?"

"Yes. … Very well. … He chose the business world. … He was always in deep competition with Dr. Danner, as I recall."

"That's an understatement, Doctor."

"By that remark, … you answer a lot of my questions about you, Jonathan."

"Yes. … That seems to be the story of my life, … why I am so driven, … so competitive."

"Nothing wrong with that. It breeds nothing but success."

"Let me get right to the point of my visit with you."

"I'm listening, Jonathan."

"My belief system … is … being challenged."

"Can you elaborate?"

"Do you … know about the *psychic lady*?"

"Certainly. … I have heard about her, … as most of our group has."

"What do you know?"

"That she is controversial, … but … I haven't investigated *why* that is."

"Well, … *that* is what I have been assigned to do, … as my first project at Superior General."

"That's interesting."

"Dr. Danner believes … she … is a fraud, and … he wants me to debunk her. That's my assignment."

"And so?"

"That's … NOT what is happening, Doctor."

"Let me read into this a little bit. … You … think she could be for real?"

"That's putting it into layman's terms."

"I'm seeing the picture now. … Interesting. … Very interesting. … I need to investigate this deeper … before we continue. … Can we postpone the rest of our discussion until tomorrow, Jonathan?"

"Of course."

(the next day …)

JONATHAN AND THE SECOND OPINION

"Son, … you're asking questions that … seekers have been searching for the answers to since the beginning of time."

"Yes. … My mind has been quite busy driving me … crazy … in my search for answers."

"All I can do for you … is … share my findings. … I have not reached any conclusions as to their truthfulness, Jonathan."

"I have self-analyzed *my* situation."

"And your conclusion?"

"I am suffering … either from a dose of a … new reality … or … I've become delusional."

"Well, … that certainly is interesting, isn't it? … What questions are you seeking answers to?"

"Like, … what is *this* all about, Doctor?"

"I'm assuming you're talking about life … in general?"

"Yes. … That … and … *why* we are here."

"Perhaps, we are just … *entertainment* … for a *bored creator*."

"Are you serious?"

"Not as outlandish as it seems, Jonathan. … Are you *really* here … talking to me?"

"Yes, … I know I am, … if that is a serious question; … or … at least I *believe* I am."

"Well, … if you know anything about science, … you realize that WE … should not exist."

"Yes, Doctor, … I know about that hypothesis."

"Do you want me to continue?"

"I follow you so far. … Please continue."

"There are theories about different dimensions, … for example String Theory, … the Multiverse Hypothesis, … etc, … etc. … And on and on. … And then there is this thing we all do … called … sleeping and dreaming. What is that all about? … Plus, … some mystics believe that we exist in a dream when we think we are awake. … Also, … did you know that our current scientific knowledge … supports … the theory of time travel?"

"I think I remember reading about that in my studies."

"Well, … if that's true, … then you could be confronting something like that … with the lady."

"I am having a hard time grasping all this, Doctor."

"I know, my boy. … This is all hypothetical. … You like puzzles. … See if you can meet the challenge before you."

"It's a challenge to me, alright. … But … I see where you're going with this. … I need to be open minded."

"That's my suggestion, Jonathan."

"Thank you, Doctor."

FOURTH CHILD

"That's just the point I am trying to make here, Ana. … They are all just stories that are blown out of proportion."

"Well, Kathie, … the story I am interested in is the story about the doctors that visited her, … all four doctors at once."

"Oh, yes. I heard that story. She supposedly gave the wrong answer."

"Do you know that story?"

"Yes. … I'll tell you as I heard it. I don't know which doctor she was referring to, but supposedly she was uncanny accurate about everything she told them; *except* … she said he had four children, and he took that as proof that she was not valid as he stated he only has *three* children."

"That's the story I am interested in."

"Why are you so interested, Ana?"

"Because, … and here's the surprise, … I *could* be the *fourth* child that he doesn't know about."

"Oh!!"

ANA WANTS TO KNOW

"Ana. Ana. Why do you *still* persist in wanting to know about the lady?"

"Like I told you, Kathie, … I am still investigating. … I need answers. … Ok?"

"What is it that you want to know? ………. If I tell you what I know or heard, will you drop this subject? … It can only cause trouble."

"Please, just tell me."

"The story, as I heard it, … is that they found this unconscious woman at the Catholic cemetery and brought her here to our hospital where she was put on life support or something like that."

"I'm listening."

"She remained unconscious until one day ….."

"One day, what, Kathie?"

"A nurse found her sitting up in bed just staring at her every move."

"And … ?"

"And as the nurse told it, … she approached the lady and expressed her delight that she was awake, … saying something like *welcome back to the world*."

"And … ?"

"The lady spoke and said, 'Who am I, and where am I?' Nurse Karen replied that she was at Superior General Hospital and asked her if she knew who she was. The lady replied *no, she didn't, but the nurse should know her because she,* the lady, *knows her,* the nurse, *very well.*"

"Wow. What happened then, Kathie?"

"The nurse, … caught off guard, said that the lady *couldn't* know her because that was the nurse's first day here and her first time in her room. However, … the lady said the nurse was married to John McDoad, and had two children by a previous marriage. She said the nurse had two brothers and a sister and that the nurse was having an affair with one of the doctors here. … The lady then highly advised the nurse to stop the affair immediately."

"That's the same story your office staff was telling me, Kathie."

"Yes. I have heard it so many times I have it memorized. … And yes, … as expected, Nurse Karen was so embarrassed that she resigned the following day."

"Don't you find that fascinating?"

"All the many stories are, but that doesn't mean that they are *true*, Ana. People embellish. You know better than to believe in that psychic stuff."

KATHIE AND ANA

"Well, Ana, this is a lot of reminiscing we have to do. Those were the good old days."

"Well, we're not *that* old, Kathie."

"Are you kidding? … You're going to be twenty five."

"And you're already twenty five. How does it feel to be *old*?"

"What is this thing about that fancy box I have been holding for you all this time, Ana?"

"Yes. Let me see it. I want to see what it looks like. I haven't seen that box for years."

"It's in that cabinet over there. ….."

"Wow. It's gorgeous. I didn't remember how beautiful it was, Kathie. Look at all that delicate carving."

"How do you open it, Ana?"

"That's the secret. I have to take it to the lawyer on my 25th birthday."

"Well, that's a little strange, don't you think?"

"Yes, … but my whole life is … not what I thought it was. … Don't you agree?"

"Well, I'm certainly curious about this box. What do you make of it?"

"Well, I don't remember. … Did it come with a key?"

"No. Just this box, Ana."

"Well, I bet the lawyer has the key. … We'll just have to wait and see on my birthday. … What's the matter, Kathie?"

"This all is very overwhelming. … I'm kind of in shock."

"I know. I know. Me too. … Do you want me to do this on my own?"

"Of course not. No. No. … No way. … But I want to go over this again, Ana."

"What is it you want to know, Kathie?"

"Are you sure about all this, Ana?"

"Ok … I'm going to tell you something that I'm not supposed to tell anyone. … Can you keep a secret, Kathie?"

"I'm going to bop you … if you keep this up, Ana."

"No. … I'm serious. … I mean, *really* serious. … I'm in *very* deep."

"What in the heck are you getting at?"

"I hired a detective agency, … but … not your *ordinary* kind of agency."

"What does all *that* mean? … *a very secret sort of agency?*"

"They … actually contacted *me*."

"They contacted you? … Why, Ana?"

"I think it has something to do with my rich uncle. … You know my aunt's husband? … He was involved in some … possibly sordid things."

"This is getting very strange and weird, Ana."

"Like I said, … you don't have to ……."

"I'm in. I'm in. … I can't help but be a little vocal. … Bear with me. … Go on, Ana."

"Well, … when they contacted me, it was by an agent showing up at my door in Athens. First, I was scared and … very apprehensive, but … he assured me he was there looking out for *my* best interests."

"How did you know that he wasn't an assassin … or something?"

"Believe me, Kathie, … first I was scared. He told me to meet him in a public place so that I would feel safe."

"And … did you do that?"

"Yes. And I took some of my friends with me, … but I told them nothing."

"Go on, Ana."

"So, … we met and he showed me his law business card and asked if we could be alone, … but my friends could be close by."

"And … ?"

"Well, we talked and talked. … He knew things about me and my parents that I never knew.   After a while, I felt comfortable and sent my friends their way."

"This is quite a story you're telling me here."

"There's more, Kathie.   Lots more. … And … it is going to get weirder. … Can you handle that? ….. There is something I have to ask of you."

"Ok…. What?"

"You … have to sign something … and … take a vow."

"A … what?"

"A vow of silence."

"Are you kidding me, Ana?"

"No. … And I'm being serious. Very serious."

"You had better explain this to me. … What have you gotten yourself into?"

"I'll tell you, Kathie, and … you … can back out after you know."

"Wow. Wow. Wow! … You can understand why I'm concerned can't you?"

"Ok, Kathie, … here goes. … It was explained to me that this is a very exclusive agency, … like the CIA … or FBI … or Interpol. … They have access to everything that is available, … but you and me? … We have to have clearance … and … be aware of its secrecy and … be in agreement with all its perks. … and … dangers."

"There are dangers?"

"Not as long as we abide by the rules."

"Wow. Wow! … Ana, … are you sure??"

"I can't share anything with you … unless you're in. ….. Hand me that briefcase over there by the door, Kathie."

"What do you want me to do with those folders?"

"Read them … carefully … and initial each page."

"What is this?"

"I anticipated that you would accept, … and … you have already been thoroughly investigated for the last three months. … All you have to do is read and sign. I'll notarize it."

"I guess you know me as well as I know you."

"Sisters through and through, … right?"

"Right."

THE NEW RESIDENCE

"Ana, I'm very excited to tell you about our new residence."

"Well, you certainly have created a fantasy wonderland in my mind about that place, Kathie."

"I can't wait for you to actually see for yourself where we will be living! It's luxury living at its best."

"So. … How expensive is this place?"

"Oh. It's expensive alright, … but not for *us*."

"What do you mean by that, Kathie?"

"Do you remember all the pictures and brochures I sent to you?"

"I still have all of them packed away in my luggage."

"Well, listen to this … They have upgraded the complex even more. They now have what they call the *Ultimate Suite*."

"I don't see how they can improve on what I have already seen."

"I received a tour last week before you arrived, Ana. … It was stunning."

"You have my attention."

"Look at this new brochure. … What do you think?"

"Everything is so beautiful in this brochure."

"And it really *does* look just like that. … Our suite is over 4000 square feet."

"Wow. … I can't wait to actually see it, Kathie."

"BUT. … There is a catch, Ana."

"Ok. … What does *that* mean?"

"You know you're beautiful, … RIGHT?"

"NO. … I do not know that, … and now I *am* worried. What have you gotten us into?"

"It's not all that bad, … and … I knew you would go along with it. … Right?"

"Go along? ... With WHAT?"

"Well, ... let me explain it this way. ... Look at the brochures."

"I am looking, Kathie."

"What's missing, Ana?"

"I don't get where you're going with this."

"Please. Don't look so worried. ... You can easily do this."

"Just tell me what you have done."

"I signed you up as the *new* model and spokesperson, Ana."

"You what?"

"We ... take advantage of your beauty."

"Or maybe, Kathie, we find something we can afford."

(Silence ...)

"Ok. Ok. I'll do it."

"Thank you. Thank you. I knew you would come through for us, Ana."

(Later ...)

"Where are we going, Kathie?"

"Where do you think we're going? ... I'll tell you. ... To *paradise*, that's where."

"We're going to the complex?"

"Yes. Yes. Yes, ... we have an appointment. ... We have to hurry or we will be late."

"Now you have me all excited."

"You should be. You're going to love our new home, Ana."

(at UTOPIA ...)

"Wow. ... Is this the entrance?..... This is impressive, Kathie. Look at this. Flowers everywhere. This is just as beautiful as any garden I have ever seen."

"I told you. ... I told you so."

"This is like driving through a beautiful park. … Is that the complex up ahead? … It's beautiful."

"We're expected, but we still have to show our ID at the front gate….."

(the girls pass through the front gate …)

"That was easy."

"Later when we move in, Ana, we will have electronic tags that will identify us."

"Is that the pool area?"

"Yes. … And you will notice that it is stocked with … *eye candy*!"

"*Eye candy* … What is that?"

"Silly girl. Just look at all those gorgeous men."

"Oh. … That *is* a nice touch."

"And, … we have a direct view from our bedroom balconies; … and … we are equipped with binoculars."

"You have thought of everything haven't you, Kathie?"

"Nothing but the best. … Nothing but the best for you, … my best friend in the world."

"I think you're buttering me up for something."

"Ok. … Straighten up. … We're about to meet the management. ….. Hello. I am Kathie. And this is Anastacia. I apologize for being a little late."

"So nice to meet the both of you. I am Patricia Marvel, CEO of our UTOPIA. You're right on time … and, I assume this beautiful lady is our new Image at our complex?"

"Anastacia has recently arrived from overseas where she has been modeling for the leading agencies over there. … She will require some adjusting, Ms. Marvel."

"Well, … we will do everything to make her feel right at home here at UTOPIA. If you will wait here in our lobby, our full management will join us shortly."

(The girls whisper together …)

"Kathie, … what have you gotten me into?"

"Ana, … you're *already* a star around here. … Just look aloof."

"Look *aloof?* ... I must look like a *goof.* ... You should have warned me."

"Shh. Shh. Just be your elegant self, Ana."

(Later ...)

"You did surprisingly well, don't you think, Ana?"

"Because I was in shock. ... I was mortified. ... All the picture taking. ... It was a good thing you did all the talking, Kathie."

"I was a little worried. You could have blown it at any moment."

"I caught on pretty fast. ... You know how I hate all that *pretty people* stuff."

"You did excellent, Ana. Don't you think it was worth it?"

"Yes. Yes. ... I can pretend to be an elegant high-priced model ... if ... we can pull this off."

"Just keep posing for the new brochures ... and ... cozying up to the big brass, and we're in."

"I am ok with the pictures, … but … I don't know about the cozying up to the big boys. They are already a little *too* friendly, … and … they are all *married* men."

"You'll do just fine, Ana. … You already have. … I'm so glad you're ok with all this."

"You're a nutcase, but I still love you. … But, Kathie, … there are things I need to tell you. … We need to talk."

"Later. … Do you have any idea what these suites go for?"

"No. I don't have a clue, Kathie."

"I am guessing one or two million dollars."

"How many units are there?"

"The brochures say sixty units."

"Expensive, huh?"

"Yes, but we are worth it. … Right?"

"Right!"

ANASTACIA'S DIARY

Dear Diary …..

Finally. … So good to be home in America. … Paris was wonderful … and I learned a lot about life. I have my degree … my PhD. … And now my new life living with my bestest friend, Kathie. … Should I tell her? I hope she will understand. … It's down to just four. … I will find out. … I hope she doesn't get upset when I tell her we have been living a lie.

KATHIE AND ANASTACIA (THE REVEAL)

"Kathie, please sit down. I have a lot to tell you."

"Why are you being so mysterious, Ana?"

"Because, what I have to tell you is shocking."

"Well, you certainly know how to get my attention."

"I don't know how to begin, ... but you need to know this."

"I'm listening, Ana."

"We have been living a lie."

"What in heaven's name are you talking about?! I'm very worried about you. You're talking crazy."

"Kathie, please. ... Just listen. ... Hear me through. You know how we grew up as next door neighbors, right?"

"Yes, of course. It was wonderful having you as my neighbor *and* best friend."

"Did it ever make you wonder *why* our houses were built so close together?"

"That's all I ever knew. So … I never thought about it, Ana."

"Neither one of us ever gave it a second thought that there were just the two houses and no other houses for miles around. … Right?"

"So. What's your point, Ana?"

"Just keep listening."

"Believe me. I'm listening."

"Did you know our parents worked for my uncle, William Masterson??"

"I never gave that a moment's thought. And … so what if they did?"

"Just keep listening. There are things you don't know."

"Ok. Ok. It's about time I tell *you* something, Ana."

"No. Let me finish my story first."

"No. No, Ana. I think I know what you're about to tell me, and … I already know. I need to confess something to you."

"How could you know what I'm about to tell you, Kathie?"

"Because … I had to *promise* never to tell you."

"What?! What were you never supposed to tell me?!"

"No. No. Never mind. Go on with *your* story, Ana."

"Wait a minute. What are you saying *you* know?"

"Well. Let's hear what you have to say, … and we'll see if I know."

"Kathie, did you know my mother is *not* … my *biological* mother? And … my father is *not* my *biological* father?"

"Yes. I knew that, Ana."

"What!… WHAT!! You … knew I was adopted and … you never let on that you knew that?!"

"Ok. Ok. … I was wrong. … But … I was told from the earliest age I can remember that … if… you found out, you would be terribly hurt, … and … I should always keep you from finding out."

"Wow! … WOW!! … This changes everything. And I thought I was revealing the secret to *you*. Boy, oh boy. … I need to rethink this. ………. Kathie, remember I told you about that special detective agency, and I had you sign those papers and promise to abide by their rules??"

"Yes. I remember all that very well, Ana. ... What did you find out from your detectives?"

"Well. ... You knew my uncle was rich. ... *very* ... *very* ... *rich!!*"

"Yes. I was told that he paid for and provided everything including our two houses. And everybody's salary and all our needs."

"You knew that, Kathie?"

"Yes. And. ... I was told that if you found out, Ana, ... it ... would all stop and ... I would be to blame. I couldn't stand the thought of *being to blame*."

"Wow! That explains everything. You *knew* my mother and her twin sister?"

"Yes, Ana. They were both very beautiful. You couldn't tell them apart. I couldn't understand how *you* could look so much like them if you were adopted."

"Well, then you *really* don't know everything."

"What do you mean by that, Ana?"

"Ok. Let me explain what I found out."

"Please do. I'm confused."

"You only know half the story, Kathie. You know that my uncle was rich. Very, very, *very*, rich."

"Yes, I surmised that."

"He married my aunt. My mother's twin sister."

"Ok … I'm following your story."

"My uncle does *not* like children, and he doesn't want anything to do with children. Are you following me so far?"

"Ok, Ana. I think so."

"So, my aunt agreed to ….."

"Not to have children. … Right?"

"Not exactly."

"Please explain, Ana."

"She was pregnant when they met, but he still fell in love with my aunt. Madly in love."

"Oh. Now I'm starting to get the picture."

"There were conditions. … He would provide a very good life for her offspring. … a very, *very* good life."

"So, … your uncle is our benefactor."

"Kathie, do you get it now?"

"No. No. Not really."

"Well. … The bottom line is I want to find my *biological* father."

"Whoa! Back up, Ana! This is totally confusing."

"Don't you get it? My mother is *not* my mother. She is the *twin* sister to my *biological* mother!"

"So. … Your real mother is … your *aunt* ?!"

"Yes. Yes! Do you get it now?"

"I think so, Ana. Maybe. So. Who is your *father* ?"

"*That* is what I am after. And, … I think I am a *sperm donor baby* !"

"What does that mean, Ana?"

"That is a complicated question to answer right now. But, I think I have narrowed the search down to one of four doctors residing at this hospital. They were all donors in the Mensa Sperm Donor Program at Harvard."

"Wow, Ana. Again, I don't know if that answered my questions or opened up new questions."

"Will you help me, Kathie?"

"Of course I will."

OK. WHAT HAPPENED?

"It's about time. Why did you *not* answer your phone, Ana?"

"Because it is sitting over there where I accidentally left it."

"Oh my gosh. I never noticed it there. I'm sorry."

"Well. … Aren't you going to question me, Kathie?"

"You're upset aren't you, Ana?"

"Yes!"

"It did not go well. … Huh."

"It was unbelievable."

"I am listening, Ana."

"I don't know how to tell you."

"Just tell me."

"NOTHING!"

"What does that mean?"

"Just what I said. ... NOTHING."

"You're saying, ... there was *nothing* ... IN THE BOX?"

"I turned it upside down to be sure. ... I even shook it, Kathie."

"That is *unbelievable* !"

"I am in shock. ... I really am."

"I understand, Ana."

THE INHERITANCE

"Kathie, it seems my inheritance may never see the light of day, so to speak."

"Ana, I'm so sorry. … What happened?"

"My lawyer rather reluctantly explained to me that my aunt, or my new found biological mother, was a beautiful front for espionage."

"What!? … Are you purposely trying to confuse me?"

"I am trying to become *unconfused* myself. … It seems that my uncle was a SPY!"

"Are you kidding me, Ana?"

"No, Kathie, I am serious. … The lawyer felt an obligation to divulge all the secret goings on to me."

"So what did he tell you?"

"He revealed a side I never knew about my uncle."

"I'm listening, Ana."

"It seems that it wasn't that he didn't *like* us. ... He was trying to *protect* us."

"From what?"

"The lawyer was gracious enough to explain that, because they are no longer living, I had a right to know the truth."

"And what is the *truth*?"

"That he and my biological mother removed us from the dangers of espionage, and his wealth may be *ill gotten* gains."

"So, Ana, the bottom line is you may not inherit anything."

"That, Kathie, is the possibility."

INFORMATION PLEASE

"Wow. Did they ever deliver, didn't they!?"

"Yes, they certainly did. … I don't know how they hid all this from us, Kathie."

"Well, all this information certainly puts a different light on dear old Uncle Masterson."

"And did you read the section *on* and *about* my *biological* mother, Kathie?"

"That's kind of hard to get used to, isn't it Ana, … *Aunt* or *Mother* ….."

"Well, it certainly puts a different perspective on things, doesn't it."

"How do your detectives get all of this information?"

"Like I first informed you, they are *more* than just a detective agency; … and we are now part of that agency, Kathie. We both signed on, and we have to abide by the rules *or else*."

"Or else what?"

"We truly don't want to find out, *do we*?"

"Ana, that sounds too scary to me."

"It's alright. … It's ok. … We will just follow the rules. We need this information. … It's all ok."

"We have to burn all of this information within three days. … We better get reading."

"Just follow the rules, Kathie."

UTOPIA'S NEW OWNERS

"Ana, what is happening? That nice lady from management was just at our door. She seemed very upset."

"She was fired or terminated because of me, Kathie."

"What!? What is going on here!? … She has always treated us so good."

"She stuck up for me when I didn't know how to react."

"You didn't know how to react to *what* ??"

"Well, Kathie, … that good-looking married office manager thought he could be inappropriate with me."

"I understand, Ana. … We don't take abuse from anybody. … We will just find us a new home."

"Kathie, I have more to tell you."

"This is upsetting … very upsetting. Why aren't *you* more upset?"

"Well, … because there is *more* to the story."

"The more I think about it, the angrier I become. I could tell something like this might happen by the way he always looked at you. ... It's all ok. ... We'll just move out."

"When he fired her right in front of me, Kathie, I just walked out; ... and he shouted after me that I would be next."

"That arrogant *you know what* ! ... I should go tell him off myself!!"

"That won't be necessary. He is not working here anymore."

"What? How did that come about?"

"Kathie, I have more to tell you. ... We have a *new* management team working here now."

"Ana, you had better explain all this to me right now. ... Do we have to move out or not??"

"Not."

"You're going to need a good bopping here, Ana."

"Ok. Ok. It's all good. I shouldn't toy with your emotions, ... but you always think the worst."

"How could things get worse? We love this place, don't we?"

"Yes, Kathie. Yes, we love this place, … and so I did something."

"You *did* something?"

"Calm down. Let me explain. Please, just let me explain."

"Why aren't you as upset as I am, Ana?"

"Because … I was gone all day yesterday for a reason. ….."

"I'm listening. … You had an appointment with your lawyer, didn't you."

"Yes, Kathie. Yes I did; and as you will recall, they had an issue with my inheritance."

"Yes, I remember that the lawyer informed you that it was being investigated for some reason and you may not receive anything."

"*That* was very worrisome to me because I owed a very very large amount to my special detective agency."

"Should we be worried? That all sounds very scary, Ana."

"Well, I informed them that I had problems with my inheritance and paying them right now ....."

"And ... ?"

"And ... *they* took care of my inheritance problem."

"What? What are you saying, Ana?"

"First of all, ... I am saying that I *fired* that SOB!"

"You *fired* that married SOB!?"

"Yes, and we now have a wonderful new management team headed by my *hero of the hour.*"

"You're talking about ....."

"Yes, Kathie. She will always be my *hero* ... and she's ecstatic about her new salary and living arrangements."

"But o*ur* UTOPIA, Ana?? ... *Our* ... UTOPIA??"

"Yes, YES, Kathie. The first thing I did with my inheritance money was purchase UTOPIA; and, of course, pay our special detectives for their excellent work. ... And it *did* take 10 - 12% of my inheritance to purchase UTOPIA, ... so we *do* have a little money left over for renovations."

"Yes, Ana, … and I know how you *love* to renovate."

"And I know how *you* love UTOPIA, Kathie."

"Life is good."

"And a little crazy, huh?"

SECTION THREE

JONATHAN AND ANA

JONATHAN MEETS ANASTACIA

"Ma'am."

"Yes. May I help you?"

"I don't mean to bother you, but can I ask you a question?"

"I believe you surely can. What can I help you with?"

"I live here in this beautiful complex, and someone pointed out to me that you were one of the new owners. Am I correct?"

"What did you say your name is?"

"I'm sorry. I should have introduced myself. I'm Jonathan Masters. I'm a relatively new resident at your complex, and I am also interning at Superior General Hospital."

"So … nice to meet you, Jonathan Masters. My name is Kathrine Rothchild, and I am also employed at Superior General. You may address me as *Kathie* if you so wish."

"Please. Address me as *Jonathan*."

"So … Do you approve of our complex, Jonathan?"

"It's just magnificent. It was very nice when I first moved in, but all I can say now is … wow!!"

"Thank you for that compliment, but we owe all this to my partner. She is in charge of renovations; and boy, does she ever like to renovate!"

"Well, Kathie, tell her for me that I think she is doing an unbelievably great job."

"Why don't you tell her yourself?"

"Because …. Well, … I don't know who she is."

"What is your name again?"

"Jonathan."

"Do you like games, Jonathan?"

"I enjoy puzzles."

"It seems you also like games. Do you agree with me on that, Jonathan?"

"I'm sorry. I don't understand, Kathie."

"I know who you are, Jonathan. My girlfriend has a crush on you … and … you know it."

"I'm embarrassed. Totally embarrassed."

"Jonathan, I'm just trying to take the edge off this awkward situation. Please stay and talk with me."

"I don't know how to respond."

"Ok. Ok. Let me explain. You're very handsome. She thinks, … therefore, … you must have an ego off the charts."

"I'm very much embarrassed by the unwarranted compliments. But …. just look at her. She is the most beautiful woman I have ever seen."

"You guys are so alike. So … you *do* know … *exactly* … who I am talking about."

"You, Ma'am, … are a very clever woman. Getting me to admit that I know of her. What man wouldn't be awestruck by her beauty?"

"And just look at you. Perfect body and looks."

"Ok. It's time for me to come clean. I kind of thought she was looking at me through those binoculars. So … I go to the gym every day at 8:00 AM … and … pump up my muscles to look my best … just in case."

"Ha ha. This is funny. Two shy … but *pretty people* playing games."

"Listen. I *am* very shy and awkward, … and I don't have *any* experience with women."

"I can tell by our conversation that it's too late for you … Life has just passed you by. You have lost out in the game of life, … haven't you, Jonathan?"

"Very funny. Well, you are a very different woman from any I have ever met before."

"Ok. Ok. I have to be careful here … You're going to perceive me as some sort of weirdo, aren't you?"

"I think … you may be correct there, Kathie."

"Ok. Ok. Give me another chance to become normal here … I'm more involved than you know, and I want the best for my dear friend. I just don't want you guys to blow this."

"Well, … I kind of like where you're taking this … I need all the help I can get, Kathie."

"What do you think about actually meeting her, Jonathan, and … seeing where it goes?"

"How do you propose to make that happen?"

"Well, she would literally kill me if she overheard this conversation, so … we have to be discreet."

"I wasn't kidding when I said I was shy… and that I have no experience with women. … None whatsoever …"

"And believe me. She has no real experience either. … She has never even been really properly kissed."

"Wow. This is crazy talk. I can't believe I'm going to admit it … but … it's the same for me. … Just for the record, I am a really straight guy."

"I can tell you are, … and … she is a straight shooter too."

"Ok."

"Here's the plan, Jonathan. You be at the lounge at 8:00 Friday evening. She won't be suspecting anything. … We'll come in soon after. … You come over to introduce yourself and compliment her on the renovations, … and … we'll see what happens."

"I'm already nervous."

"I'm with you, Jonathan. I think you will do just fine, … but … if you need help, just follow my lead. Ok?"

"I got it. … I understand. Kathie, … you're no longer weird in my eyes, but … extremely witty. You have made my day."

"Jonathan, we're going to be the best of friends. … See you Friday."

THE HAPPENING

"Kathie, I'm sorry I'm late. … There was a fender bender."

"Are you hurt, Ana?"

"No. It didn't involve me, but it sure slowed my getting home on time. I know how you looked forward to tonight."

"Can you hurry? They won't save our table after 8:00."

"Ok. … If you don't mind my going out looking like this … with my hair a mess and no makeup."

"It will be a good test, Ana."

"Are you going to … test … how fast I can get ready?"

"Just hurry, Ana. You can wear my new blouse."

"At least I'll be dressed nicely."

(Later ...)

"It's 8:25, Kathie. Do you think they saved our table?"

"I'll ask. ... Nope. They are very busy tonight, ... but we can stand by the bar until something opens up."

"Do you see anyone you know?"

"I see a couple of people I recognize on the dance floor. Hey, Ana. ... Look. ... Isn't that your hunk over there with his date? ... She is very pretty."

"Look how she is cuddling up to him, Kathie."

"Can you blame her? ... Look how handsome he looks."

"I think he's looking our way. ... Don't let him see us looking. ... Oh, my gosh, Kathie. ... Look what I've done to your blouse!"

"You'd better go to the bathroom, Ana, ... and rinse that out before it sets."

"Ok, but I'll probably be a while. I know you really like this blouse. I'll replace it."

"Take your time, Ana. I'm enjoying the music."

(a few minutes later …)

"Jonathan, … you saw us come in late."

"Yes, I thought you had stood me up. You have got to help me out of a tricky situation, Kathie."

"And what is that?"

"That … woman is trying to buy me a drink."

"She's not your date?"

"Of course not. I've been waiting for you to show up. I told her my date would be here shortly. … You need to be my date and back up my story. … Where did Ana go?"

"She had a mishap. She spilled her drink all over herself. She feels clumsy and embarrassed. … Would you wait here please? I'll go see how she is doing….."

(in the bathroom …)

"Ana, how are you doing here?"

"Not so good, Kathie. I think the blouse is ruined. I'm just drying it off … so I have something to wear."

"Well, you won't believe what just happened."

"Are we getting kicked out for making a mess?"

"No, Ana. It's actually good news. We have a table."

"Great! … That's what we wanted, isn't it?"

"There's a catch."

"What kind of catch?"

"A very handsome catch."

"Are you serious? … How did you pull that off, Kathie?"

"He isn't on a date. … He spotted us … and … was nice enough to offer us his table."

"Is he leaving?"

"No. No. … We will be sitting with him."

"Oh my gosh! This is terrible! I look a mess, and besides that, … I'm a clumsy doofus. … What will he think of me?"

"Just be yourself, Ana. What will be, will be."

"I can't believe this. My dream man is going to be very disappointed in me."

(a few minutes later back at the table …)

"Hi. It's nice to meet you."

"My name is Ana. … What's going on here?"

"Hello, Ana. I'm Jonathan. … It seems like we're a lot alike. I've spilled my drink all over myself too. … I hope I don't embarrass you with the way I look."

"Excuse me, Ana and Jonathan. … I'll leave you alone to talk. I have a date … with … the dance floor."

"Ana, … may I have the privilege of a dance with you? … If we dance close, … we can hide our clumsy goofs."

"Jonathan, … I believe you surely may, … and I like your creative idea."

(Later …)

"Well, well. What is that smile all about, Ana?"

"You know very well what. … That … was the *best dance* of my life, Kathie."

"That's why I left early. … He offered to take you home, … and … I knew you were in good hands."

"It couldn't have been better. … At first he was shy, … but … when I asked him if his accident was on purpose, he confessed … and that broke the ice. We laughed all night."

"So ……?"

"So, I'm happy. … So, so happy. … Unbelievably happy. … We have a date tonight."

"Sometimes *Fate* has plans."

"I'm suspicious. … *Was* it *Fate*? … or something else, Kathie?"

"I'm not confessing to anything."

FIRST DATE

"Kathie. ... Kathie. ... Wake up! I need to talk to you."

"Why are you shaking me? ... I'm awake, Ana."

"I need to tell you about last night."

"I knew it. ... It's about your big first date with Jonathan. ... Right?"

"This is serious. Are you going to listen to me or not?"

"Do I have any choice?"

"If you don't want me to bother you, I won't."

"Ok. Ok. I'm awake now, Ana. Don't be so grouchy. ... I'm listening."

"What does ... *smitten* mean?"

"You know what that is ... It's, it's ... I don't know how to explain it. I'm not all awake. Why do you ask that?"

"Because ... *he* said it."

"*How* did *he* say it? … In what manner did he say it? … Joking or serious?"

"I don't know. … I just remember I was embarrassed for some reason. … I don't remember what it means. Is it a bad thing?"

"Sure it's bad. … *You* could catch it!"

"Are you serious, Kathie?"

"Yes. … The next thing, … you stay awake all night … thinking … ; and then, … if he doesn't call, you panic; … and if and when he does call, … you're all giddy; … and everything revolves around *him*. … And it gets even worse."

"How so?"

"You start *bothering* your best friend when she needs her sleep."

"Come on, Kathie. This is serious to me."

"Ok. Ok. I'm awake now, and I *do* want a detailed report on your first date with Jonathan. Let's hear it."

"Oh. … It was wonderful. … Just wonderful!"

"Details, Ana. ... Details, please."

"When he came to pick me up, he brought me a corsage. It was like we were going to a prom, and he pinned it on my dress. ... I was afraid he would notice I was trembling. After all, he *is* the best looking man in the world!"

"Oh. Yes. Yes, I see. How could you *not* tremble?"

"And, I could see he was a little nervous also."

"You noticed that, huh?"

"I noticed everything. He is the most handsome man in the world. But ... I'm not the only one who thinks that. I could see other people looking and staring."

"You mentioned that before. Do you think they could be looking at *you* also?"

"Well, maybe a little. There was one incident I have to tell you about, Kathie."

"And what was that?"

"They asked for our autographs. It was so funny."

"Sounds like a cute story. Let's hear it."

"We were at our table at that fancy new restaurant on 5th Avenue."

"Wow! … Nothing but the finest restaurant in town for you guys."

"Shh. … Listen to my story."

"I'm listening, Ana."

"We were really getting involved in our conversation, leaning toward each other, whispering … Then, we both noticed that it seemed everyone was staring at us … and they *were!*"

"How do you know?"

"Because, all of a sudden, a little boy came running over to our table."

"A little boy came running over to your table? Why?"

"To ask for our autographs. … Can you believe that?"

"Well, this is a fascinating story. Go on. What did you do?"

"We were both startled. We didn't know what to do. … We realized right away that we were being mistaken for who knows who. It became very silent. ... Everyone was looking at us."

"What did you do?"

"We just looked at each other and started laughing."

"Jonathan threw his arms up and shouted, 'We're not anybody!' ... I stood up and shouted that that wasn't true. That 'we are somebody!' ... just not who they thought we were. At first, there was silence. Then everybody started clapping. It was so funny. Everyone was laughing."

"What about the little boy?"

"He was just standing there ... holding a napkin. I took it from him and kissed it, ... putting lipstick all over it. He was so excited. He skipped all the way back to his table. His parents were clapping and whistling. It was so much fun!"

"So, ... it sounds like you enjoyed your evening with Jonathan."

"It was the best evening ever. ... Well... *almost*."

"What do you mean by ... *almost?*"

"When he walked me to my door at the end of our perfect date …"

"Yes. … What happened, Ana?"

"Nothing!"

"Nothing. … What do you mean by that?"

"Well, … he took my hand in both of his hands and thanked me for the best evening ever and turned and walked away."

"It sounds like the perfect evening to me."

"Don't you get it, Kathie? … I fell in love with this man this evening. Madly in love. He is supposed to sweep me off my feet, … put me on his white horse, … and smother me with kisses as he rides off into the sunset …WITH ME!"

"In other words, you wanted him to kiss you."

"Yes. Yes. YES!!"

"Oh no. You're starting to cry. … Silly girl, come here."

"You always know when I need a hug, don't you?"

"What you need to realize is that this is just the beginning of something wonderful."

"Oh, I hope so."

"Ana … I *know* so."

ANASTACIA'S DIARY

Dear Diary .....

I took her advice and I did it! ..... I was taught that women are not supposed to call guys.....but.....She said that ... that ... is very old fashioned thinking,.....and ... that today it's completely acceptable ..... I was still a little uncomfortable ..... so..... She suggested that I make an excuse ... like ... I lost an earring and maybe ... it's ... in his car and wanted to know if Jonathan had found it. ..... Well, ... Dear Diary, ... it worked! ..... We have another date tonight for dinner ... Casual attire as in ... no ... tie necessary. ... But ... I had to confess to him ... that ... I used the earring bit as an excuse to call him .... Honestly. ... I think that was the best move ever. ... He said that my confession was ... wonderful to him ... and ... that he is basically shy ... and ... now he knows that I like him. ..... Things will be different ..... Life is good!!

ANASTACIA'S DIARY

Dear Diary .....

Oh my gosh. ... Oh my gosh! ..... Too much to tell ... Boy, ... did he change, and fast! ..... He brought me flowers ... and ... he was bold, ... maybe confident is a better word. ..... He acted like we were already going together ..... He seemed so proud to have me on his arm ... and ... that gave me confidence. ..... We talked and talked ... like ... we were old friends ..... It was the best evening of my life. ... Jonathan is such a gentleman ... and ... I had my first kiss ... ever !! ..... Ok.

Ok. Details ... It was soft ... and gentle ... It was wonderful ... and over way way too fast! ... More later ...

KATHIE AND ANA

"Ana, you look sad. What's the matter? How's it going with Jonathan?"

"Not so good."

"Why is that?"

"We're in love, Kathie."

"What is so bad about that?"

"Jonathan doesn't like being in love. But, … I think it's ok."

"Do you know how crazy you guys sound? Can you explain this to me a little better?"

"Well, this is the first time for Jonathan; and my only other experience was with Phil. I dated him on and off for three years."

"I remember … you liked him a lot, Ana. He was a gentleman."

"Yeah, I thought I loved him. He was so nice to me; but, in all that time, we never even kissed."

"I remember when he confessed to you that he was gay."

"Yes. That was a shocker. But, to tell the truth, I think I knew he was gay right from the start. But it's so so different with Jonathan."

"I have to ask … have you and Jonathan kissed?"

"Nothing really serious."

"So … You really *are* both virgins?"

"In so many ways."

"Well, I think that is wonderful."

"For both of us, don't you think, Kathie?"

"Well, I want to reserve that answer for later. There … is … something to say for experience."

"Well, … I don't want … *him* … to be experienced."

"So, what is the problem?"

"Jonathan is very open and honest about his feelings … So … he doesn't like all the emotions that come with being in love."

"What is he talking about?"

"He says he can't stop thinking about me …. And … he doesn't like being jealous because other men stare at me. … He says I'm *too* beautiful ….. But … just look at him. … He has a perfect body, and he is … *so* handsome that more women stare at *him* than men stare at *me*."

"Yes, … I can see you both are cursed by being one of the *beautiful people*."

"Please. Don't make fun of us. This is serious, Kathie."

"I'm sorry. I'll try to be more understanding. Go on, Ana."

"Well, he said something that hurt me."

"What was that?"

"He said I was his *first* love … and … I said first *and* last … and … he said that … we'd see about *that*. What does he mean by *that*? That hurt."

"Honey, you said he didn't like all the crazy emotions love brings. … He is just showing his true feelings. Remember, you're both dealing with emotions that most people deal with *early* in life. … When they say *crazy love*, it's true. … It's not easy being virgins to all this."

"Well, I have a lot more to tell you, Kathie…"

"I'm listening."

"Have you ever heard of the Chippendales?"

"You mean those exotic male dancers. They really are hunks who drive women crazy."

"So, you *have* heard of them, Kathie."

"Who hasn't? I almost went to one of their gigs once, but they don't let in men and I was dating that jealous guy … so … I didn't go. Anyway … what about them?"

"Well, … get this. Jonathan was invited to be one."

"How can that be? Jonathan is going to be a doctor."

"Just let me tell the story. It will all make sense."

"I'm listening, Ana."

"Jonathan earns his great body. … He works out at the gym four days a week. He does this religiously."

"So … ?"

"Well, … it seems that some of the Chippendale men go to the same gym, and they have become close friends with Jonathan."

"And?"

"And … Jonathan confessed to me."

"What did he confess?"

"He confessed that there is a Chippendale *calendar*."

"What does that have to do with Jonathan?"

"Well, it's all innocent, … but he is in all twelve months … in … different poses; … and … he felt he should tell me up front."

"Wow! … I can't wait to see that calendar, Ana!"

"Hey, … he *is* my boyfriend."

"And? … Don't tell me … *you* … don't want to see that calendar."

"I won't look at the Chippendales, … just *my* Jonathan. And the calendar was some years ago, … and…. we probably won't ever find a copy."

"How did this come about?"

"Well, the story Jonathan told me is that he had become close workout buddies with some of the dancers; … and one day they were scheduled for a photo shoot, … and … one of the six Chippendales was sick. So, he stood in as a favor to his friends."

"I think it's wonderful that he wants to confess to anything that may be controversial. … So … it seems you are leading a very interesting life from what you are used to."

"Well, … there is even more, Kathie."

"I don't think you can top what you have already told me."

"Well … try this on for size."

"I'm listening, Ana."

"We're going to do it."

"Do what? Get married?"

"No! NO! … We're not *that* serious."

"Are you trying to confuse me, Ana?"

"Ok. Let me explain. … We're both virgins, … right?"

"Ok. … I got that. … So?"

"And we think we're in love, … right?"

"Yes … and …?"

"And … so … being mature adults, … we decided we need to know if we're compatible. *Really* compatible."

"So. You want to have SEX. Is that what you're saying, Ana?"

"No. No. No. We want to have LOVE, or whatever you want to call it."

"Well, I guess most people would call it *making* love. … So, … what's the problem?"

"I don't know *how* to make love … and … I want *you* to teach me. … You have experience. … And … Jonathan's friends are going to teach him."

"This is hilarious. … just …*HILARIOUS*!! … The Chippendales … are … teaching Jonathan … and … I'm teaching you?! Ha ha! … Talk about crazy. … This is unbelievable."

"Stop making fun. … I need you to take this seriously, Kathie."

"I'm sorry. … I'm sorry. I will. I will. … Please don't be upset."

"But, you're right. … This *is* funny stuff."

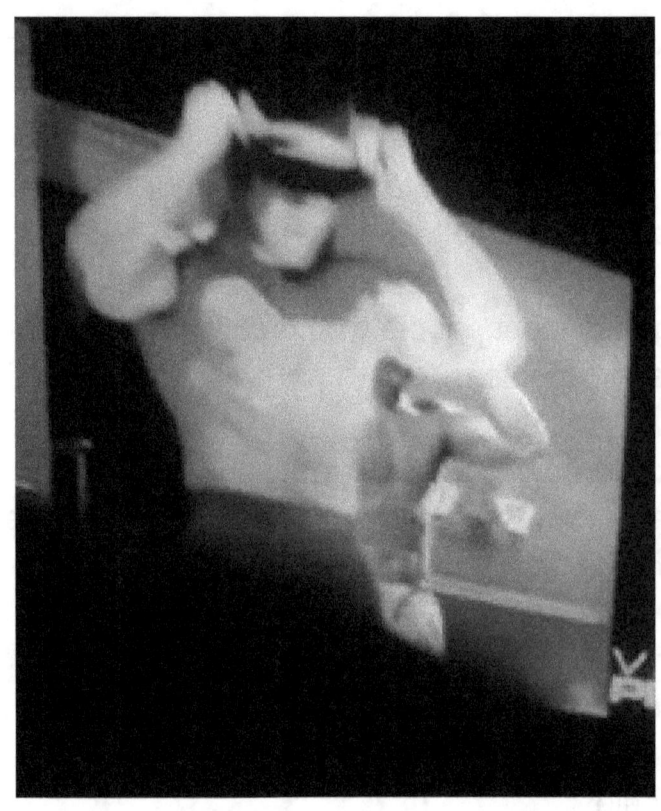

ANASTACIA'S DIARY

Dear Diary .....

This emotion is so fraught with turbulence ... so ... so ... powerful. Overwhelming with joy ... and relentless duress. ... A kiss elicits bliss. ... A touch, just as much. ... I would have it no other way ... if I have my say. ... You bring freshness without bounds to my very existence. ... Oh Jonathan ... my perfect person ... you have burrowed so deep into my very soul. ... I feel I couldn't properly exist without your love. ... I tremble ... I shake as relentless thoughts bombard my waking moments. ...

YOU have arrived. ... I would have it no other way, my perfect person. ... What is happening here? ... Emotions abide that never before existed within me. ... I awake, ... I go to sleep, ... I day dream; ... I live for your presence, ... your nearness, ... your closeness, ... the sight of you, ... the touch from you, ... the thought of you. ... You ... you ... just you. I would have it no other way, my perfect person.

JONATHAN'S DISCOVERY

"Jonathan, I have a question to ask you."

"And what question is that, Kathie?"

"What do you think of Anastacia's obsession with finding her *biological* father?"

"Well, she certainly is obsessed alright, … but I can see where she is coming from."

"She has told me that you're onboard with helping her, Jonathan."

"Of course I am. I love that woman; and anything I can do to help, I would be glad to do."

"Well, … she *is* reluctant to ask for your help in *certain* areas."

"What are you talking about, Kathie?"

"Well, … it seems your father was a part of that special Mensa program at Harvard."

"I never really knew much about that program."

"Well, … Ana has come to believe that she … is a *Mensa sperm donor baby*. So, … she needs to investigate … and find out if it's true. … Jonathan, … your father *could* know all about that program. He was very much a part of that whole group."

"I *see* where you're going, Kathie."

"Yes. We have heard all the stories of how he was so driven to see you excel."

"Yes. And I love my dad for all he has done for me."

"We heard you're going home for a visit soon."

"It's more than a visit. … Dad is very sick, and I'm very concerned about that."

"Well, … do you think you could ask some questions about that Mensa program for Ana?"

"Yes. I believe Dad would be glad to tell me what he knows, … if anything."

"Ana will be so pleased that you're being helpful in her pursuit."

"Well, … in that case, I will make it my priority to find out all that I can."

"That would be wonderful, Jonathan."

JONATHAN AND HIS DAD

"Jonathan, Jonathan. … Your mother and I are so glad you could come for a visit. It makes us so happy."

"Well, Dad, I'm glad to be here. I miss you and Mom more than I can say. … I can only stay for a few days. Dr. Danner keeps me busy."

"How is my old buddy these days?"

"He wants me to thank you, again, for funding the new trauma unit. It is beautiful and has all the latest equipment."

"Only the best for my dear friend and his hospital. So, how are you fitting in, Jonathan?"

"Dad, it couldn't be better. Dr. Danner treats me like family. I have met his whole clan, and it's unbelievable how easily I fit in."

"That makes me very very happy. Your mother and I couldn't be more pleased."

"But, Dad, how are *you* doing? I *am* concerned."

"My health is a little shaky, … but my business couldn't be better. We are the leading company on the stock exchange. … I may have to fund another wing to get rid of some money."

"That's funny, Dad. You always were a genius in the business world."

"Yes, I am proud of my business success; but I'm *more* proud of you, my boy, than any of that."

"Thank you, Dad. Thank you. If you're proud of me, that's all that matters."

"I couldn't be more proud."

"Dad, are you up to talking a little about your past?"

"Whatever do you mean?"

"I have my reasons."

"What do you want to know, Jonathan?"

"I want you to tell me about the Mensa Sperm Donor Program."

(Silence …)

"Dad! Are you alright? … You look shaken. … Please sit down."

"I'm ok. … I'm alright."

"What's the matter?"

"I knew this day would come, Jonathan."

"Dad. Dad. I'm concerned. … You don't look so good."

"Son, just give me a moment. … We *will* talk. … I need to talk to your mother about this. … She needs to be in on it."

"Dad, I don't understand. … I didn't mean to upset you."

"No, no. … You need to know. … You need to know *everything*. … We will talk. …I just need to rest a little."

"Mother! Mother, call 911!! ……"

(a few days later …)

"Jonathan, I'm so sorry about your father."

"Yes. … It was so sudden. … I'm going to need a little time to myself."

"Of course. ... Of course. ... Just know we are there for you."

"I know you are. ... Thank you all. ... I'll be ok. ... I'll be in touch. ... Tell the staff the flowers are beautiful and the ceremony was wonderful. ... Dr. Danner flew in and gave a wonderful eulogy."

"Yes. As soon as he heard, he was on his way down there. ... He was visibly very upset. ... They must have been *very* close friends."

"In his eulogy for my father, he addressed him as his brother and best friend. It was very touching. ... Not a dry eye at the service."

"That is wonderful, Jonathan."

"I have questions for my mother. ... So, ... I have to choose the right time to talk with her."

JONATHAN AND HIS MOTHER

"Mother, how are *you* doing?"

"Jonathan, ... it was too sudden."

"I know, Mother, ... I know."

"Jonathan, … I know you want to talk to me, … don't you?"

"Whenever you're ready, Mother."

"We never meant to keep it a secret from you."

"I'm listening."

"Did your father tell you anything?"

"No, … and I'm afraid I upset him."

"He always knew he would someday have to tell you."

"Mother, … I'm confused. … What are you talking about?"

"That Mensa Sperm Donor Program."

"Yes. … I wanted to question Dad about that program. … on behalf of my girlfriend. … She thinks she is a product of that program."

"Oh my gosh. Oh my gosh. He thought you knew. … That's ironic. That's … just ironic."

"Mother, … what are you talking about?"

"Son, … I can't talk right now. … I have to think this through."

"Oh Mother. … I don't want you to get upset."

"I'll be alright. … Like I said, … I need to think this through."

"I understand. … Calm down. … Please don't be upset."

(Jonathan and his mother finally talk …)

"Mother, … I'll be going back tomorrow."

"Jonathan, … Jonathan. … Oh Jonathan. … Come sit down next to me."

"Are you ok, Mom?"

"I'm not good at this sort of thing. … Your dad should have told you."

"Mom, … Are you ok? … I don't want you to get upset again."

"Just sit with me for a moment, … so I can figure out how to do this."

"Do what?"

"Talk to you. … Tell you the truth."

"Tell me *the truth*?"

"You know your dad loved you dearly."

"Yes, … of course I know that. … So?"

"So, … he always wanted to tell you."

"Mother, … now you're upsetting *me*. … Just tell me what you have to tell me. … PLEASE."

"You're a … *Mensa sperm donor baby.*"

"What! … WHAT!! … Mother, … have you gone crazy?!"

"Jonathan, … Sit back down. … This is very, very hard for me."

"I don't get it. … I just don't get it. … What are you saying to me?"

"Jonathan, Jonathan, … just calm down. … Sit down. … This has to be told."

"Mother, I don't believe you. … No! No! … NO!!"

"Please Jonathan, … just listen. … Just listen to me. … Please. Please. … PLEASE."

"I don't believe this, Mother. ... I don't believe this is happening to me."

"You have to listen to our story. ... Ok. ... Please?"

"I'll try. ... I'll try. ... But I *am* upset. ... *Very VERY* upset."

"Do you want to wait until later?"

"No. No. ... Let's get this over with."

"Are you sure?"

"Yes. Yes. ... Mother, just talk to me."

"Ok. ... I just wish your father were here."

"So do I. Believe me, ... so do I."

"Ok. ... We both need to calm down. ... Promise not to interrupt me, ok?"

"Ok. Just get on with it."

"Well, Jonathan, ... your father and I were always very much in love; and we married in our freshman year. ... We wanted children, ... but ... your father tested to be infertile and couldn't be a biological father. ... So when that Mensa program came around, … your father decided to obtain some Mensa sperm so we could produce you."

"So, … you're saying …I'm a *Mensa Sperm Donor Baby?*"

"Yes."

"Mother, … I have to go. … Thank you for the honesty."

"Jonathan, … I hope you forgive us."

"Mother, … there's nothing to forgive. … I am here thanks to the two of you and the Mensa program.   I'll be in touch."

I COULD BE YOUR BROTHER

"Jonathan, … will you please return my call? … This is Kathie."

"Kathie, what is happening with your call to Jonathan?"

"He doesn't pick up, Ana."

"He's been back for days now. … Why is he avoiding us?"

"You shouldn't have asked him for his help."

"What do you think his father told him before his passing, Kathie?"

"I don't know. … It's kind of baffling."

"I'm going over to his residence."

"No, no, no. … Let him do his thing. … He will contact us when he is ready, Ana."

"His father must have told him something awful."

"Don't go there. … It will do you no good, Ana."

"But Kathie, I'm worried. … Very worried."

(Ana finally contacts Jonathan ...)

"Jonathan, ... you answered. ... Do you want to talk?"

"I'm sorry. ... I apologize, Ana. ... I should have been straight with you from the beginning."

"Jonathan, ... what are you talking about?"

"It's still hard for me to think about."

"Are you ok?"

"Am I *ok*? ... No, no. ... I am *not* ok. ... But, ... you know, ... I have to tell you."

"Jonathan, ... you're not making any sense."

"I know, ... I know, Ana. ... I'm confused."

"If this isn't a good time for you to talk ....."

"No time ... is ... a good time to say ... what I have to say."

"What are you trying to say here?"

"Ana, ... I could be your BROTHER."

"What? … What are you saying?"

"I can't see you for a while, … until I work this out. … Goodbye, Ana."

"No, no, NO. … Please don't hang up."

CLICK.

BEST FRIENDS

"I need to talk to someone and, … you're my best friend in the world, Kathie. Can I trust you?"

"You know, sometimes you say the stupidest things. … Of course you can trust me, Ana. And it greatly offends me when you question my loyalty to you."

"I'm sorry. I know I can trust you. I'm just going through some very disturbing things right now."

"Honey, don't cry. … I guess I can be a little too strong with you sometimes. … I'll try to be a little less defensive, ok?"

"Thank you, Kathie. It would help if ……."

"Yes, I know. I'll just listen to what you have to say, Ana."

"Ok. I'll just calm down for a minute and regain my composure. Ok?"

"Yes, honey. Take your time. I'm here for you."

"Ok. Here goes."

"I'm listening, Ana."

"You know that I have the very best detectives working on my case."

"Yes. I know about that."

"You know that they give me very extensive monthly reports."

"I didn't know that they were that regular, but go on."

"Well, … I have given them permission to broaden their investigation, Kathie."

"What do you mean, Ana?"

"They are to give me reports and information about everybody I know."

"Everybody? Even me?"

"Yes, Kathie, but don't worry; I haven't read your report."

"Well, … I want to read what they found out about me, Ana."

"Later. For now, just listen to me. … You know how deeply involved I am with Jonathan."

"Yes. I know you're really head over heels in love with this man."

"Yes, that's right, but ... I feel like I've lost it. I've heard about how devastating, ... how   wonderful, ... and how crazy, love can make you. Well, ... I'm in heaven one minute and hell the next."

"Honey, so where are you now?"

"HELL!"

"Shh! Not so loud. This is a private conversation after all."

"I don't care, Kathie. I'm in hell ... hell ... HELL!"

"Ok, ok. ... But I'm going to walk away and leave you alone if you don't calm down here, Ana."

"See?! ... I'm losing it. ... I really am!"

"Hush. ... Just stop crying. ... Take a few deep breaths. ... I'm here for you. ... That's better. You're going to be alright. Just sit back and relax. ... Good. ... Much better. I'm here for you."

"Thank you. ... What would I do if I didn't have you, Kathie?"

"But, you *do* have me. ... When you're ready, let's hear about your reports."

"What I found out is devastating."

"What's devastating, Ana?"

"I'll just come out and say it."

"Ok. Please. ... Tell me."

"He ... is my *brother*!"

"You don't have any brothers, Ana."

"That's what I thought. ... But no. ... Jonathan is my brother!!"

"You really have lost it. ... You're talking crazy."

"No. ... Jonathan could be right. ... It's in the report."

"What's in this report?"

"Here. ... Read it for yourself, Kathie."

"There are too many pages here. Just tell me. ... Ok?"

"We're both the product of that Mensa Sperm Donor Program. It's all in this report."

"So. You're saying you both have been conceived from that ... Mensa Sperm Donor Program, ... correct?"

"That's what it says. ... Same sperm. ... Same father."

"I get the picture. I see the whole picture here. ... I thought you were so intelligent. ... I guess I was wrong."

"Please. ... I am already upset. ... I thought you were there for me?"

"Listen. ... Just listen for a moment, Ana."

"Ok. Ok. I'm listening, Kathie."

"Jonathan is *not* for sure your so-called *brother.* There were many sperm donors in that program, ... and you're jumping to unwarranted conclusions."

"Ok. You're right. You're absolutely right. Ok alright, ... I haven't been thinking straight. You're right, Ok? I love you, Kathie. Maybe there *is* hope."

"Yes, my dear. The odds are on your side; but, I agree, ... we need confirmation."

"But there is hope … right? I have not been thinking too clearly lately."

"I will have to agree with *that* conclusion."

JONATHAN AND KATHIE

"Jonathan, it's Kathie. If you ever cared anything for Ana, you will return my call."

"I received your message. Has something happened to Ana?"

"Jonathan, we need to talk and not over the phone. Can you meet me at Leo's Grill?"

"I don't want to be indifferent, Kathie, … but … I think it's best if we ….."

"Stop. Stop right there. This is not the time to be noble. … You need to hear what I have to say, and then you can decide what we should do or not do."

"Can I ask why you're so involved?"

"Because. I'm Ana's best friend and I can see both sides, … and I know something that's very important. And you should know about it too. You, Jonathan, deserve to have your say in what to do, … and I don't want to say anything more on the phone. Please just trust me. You really need to know."

"Ok. Ok. I hear you. I apologize for acting so weird. I think I'm losing it too. I have never been in love before, and my emotions are out of control. … I really don't know how to handle this."

"Jonathan, I'm really here to just help. Ana is going through this way worse than you can imagine. … I am so worried that this is becoming a life or death situation."

"Are you serious, Kathie?"

"You need to see for yourself."

"Kathie, … you have me trembling. … You have no idea how much I love Ana."

"Be at Leo's tomorrow evening at 6:00."

AT LEO'S

"Jonathan, you're early. I didn't expect you to be here already. Give me a hug."

"Well, thanks to your pre-talk, Kathie, I spent the night dealing with a barrage of crazy crazy thoughts about the right way to deal with this."

"Jonathan, I think you need to gather the facts and then draw your joint conclusions."

"Listening to you talk, Kathie, I'm grateful that you are onboard with us."

"Jonathan, I wouldn't want it any other way. So, … is it ok with *you* ?"

"I'm fully on board, Kathie."

"Ok then. Let's lay out the facts as we know them."

"Ok."

"First, we believe both of you were conceived from the elite Mensa Sperm Donor Program. Is that right, Jonathan?"

"And that's where my mind goes crazy. … Too many moral issues here."

"Jonathan, we want to deal with facts and only facts. … Don't you think you're getting ahead of the game?"

"The fact is, … as I see it, … that I could be sleeping with my *sister*. … That's how my mind works, and it's driving me absolutely crazy."

"Ok. Ok Jonathan. I get it. I get it. … But, … and it's a *big* but, … what if she isn't your sister or half-sister?"

"Don't you see? Until I know for sure, … I'll be going crazy, Kathie."

"That's why I'm here."

"That's why I should hightail it out of the picture before it gets any more complicated."

"Ok, Jonathan, … here it comes. … It already *is* complicated."

"What are you implying? … Are you sure?"

"Two months in. Are you going to abandon her?"

"No. No. Of course not. … Is she thinking of ….."

"No, Jonathan. … Abortion is out of the question. … That would violate her sense of spirituality."

"Good. Great. ... I'll fully support her decision. ... Well, I guess that stops all thoughts of running away."

"Jonathan, I hoped you would react just as you have. ... I am so relieved. ... What are you thinking right now?"

"Do you really want to know, Kathie?"

"Yes, let's hear your thoughts."

"When you introduced me to Ana, I was awestruck by how beautiful she is; ... and when we conversed on our first date, I realized how intelligent she is. It right away became apparent we were more than compatible. ... It was the first time for me. ... I have never felt true happiness before. ... Love is so powerful."

"Jonathan, I want to hear your story. I have time. Do you mind?"

"Kathie, ... you remind me of a therapist I dealt with in my college years."

"Well, ... I have credentials. ... I studied to be a therapist and graduated second in my class."

"Do we have time for this?"

"We have all the time in the world. Let's hear your story, Jonathan."

"Well, I don't know if you knew that in college my dad was roommate and best friends with Dr. Danner, the head of the hospital."

"I had heard that, yes."

"And it seems that Dad and Dr. Danner had this great competitive obsession with everything they endeavored to do. Dr. Danner graduated number one, and of course Dad was number two. … I did not know it at the time, but I realize it now. … That is why my dad was so determined that I achieve the number one spot in everything I did. … There was no way I was going to let him down. … I did nothing but learn and study just to please him; and I did it. I achieved his goal."

"How do you feel about that?"

"How do I feel about that, Kathie? … Good question."

"You don't have to answer that."

"No. No. I want to. Well, … I really never thought about it much; and I did, … I really did, finally figured it out. … And yes, I am glad my father pushed so hard. … I hope this doesn't sound too boastful, … but being number one from Harvard is a great honor. And yes, … I would do it all over again… the same way."

"An honest answer. … A great answer, … and that explains some things."

"Like what, Kathie?"

"Well,…. you have got to know that you are extremely good looking. … Definitely *movie star good looks*. … You probably could have any woman you went after."

"Kathie, … just a simple answer to that. … No time for anything, but going after my father's dream."

"Was it worth it, Jonathan?"

"I would like to believe that *Fate* had better plans for me."

"Well, … we'll see about that, won't we? And, just so you know, … Dr. Danner was bragging about this number one Harvard graduate who would be interning at his hospital."

"That solves a puzzle. ... I wondered why everyone acted like they knew me."

"Well, ... you were not what we expected."

"Please. .. Don't start with the *movie star good looks* spiel again."

"Well, ... let's talk about Ana."

"Kathie, ... have you talked to Ana?"

"All the time."

"Well, ... then you know she doesn't want anything to do with me."

"Where did you come up with that idea, Jonathan?"

"I confronted her ... when I was in New York on Dr. Danner's business. I went to lunch by myself, and there she was, ... just sitting, ... looking as beautiful as always reading the menu. I debated with myself for some time before I decided to just do it."

"What happened?"

"I went over and stood right in front of her. She looked up, startled to see me I guess. I asked her if I could talk to her. … For a second she didn't say anything; and then with disgust she said that she didn't even know me, … and … would I please leave."

"What then?"

"I turned and left. … I was beyond hurt. … She made it very clear … she didn't know me anymore."

"Are you sure it was Ana?"

"Of course it was Ana. … She is one of a kind. … Her beauty stands out."

"When was this, Jonathan?"

"Two weekends ago."

"Impossible. … You know we live together. … I've been trying to get her to go out with me to no avail. … She looks terrible and she knows it. … I know for a fact it wasn't her who you saw."

"You're wrong. I know what Ana looks like; … and she looked like she always does, … beautiful."

"Jonathan, do you think there are *doppelgangers* out there?"

"I was sure that was her, … but I *did* wonder why she had cut her beautiful long hair."

"Jonathan, … she still has long hair."

"I'm confused. Totally confused, Kathie. Could I have been mistaken? She looked exactly like Ana, except with short hair."

"Jonathan, hair doesn't grow that fast. See for yourself. … I took this picture last night."

"That's Ana?"

"She looks pretty bad, … huh?"

"She has long long hair in this picture. … I'm confused."

"Well, … the real question is ….."

"Yes, yes. … I love Ana. I'm totally here for her if she wants me. … I'm so sorry if I caused her to be upset."

"Jonathan, she is way beyond upset. ... She is losing a lot of weight."

"What should I do? ... What do you want me to do, Kathie?"

"Jonathan, ... just knowing that you are concerned ....."

"I'm more than concerned. I've got to go to her. Where is she?"

"Slow down. Slow down boy. She won't see you. ... I know her. ... Not the way she looks now."

"I don't care how she looks. ... I have been devastated too. Look, I'm shaking. ... Look at me. I've lost 20 pounds. I can't sleep. I can't eat. Just look at me. ... Red eyes from crying and no sleep. ... I'm a mess."

"You're in love, Jonathan. ... I'm not trying to be funny, ... but you really could use a little sprucing up."

"I've been acting crazy. ... I realize that now. ... I've been stupid, ... stupid, ... stupid."

"Jonathan, hold on. Hold on. It's time to be rational. Love and all this drama has set both of you over the edge."

"Ok. I'm listening. I'm calming down."

"You're still shaking."

"Yes, … but I feel better knowing that she still cares about me."

"Jonathan, you have a woman who is *so* in love with you."

"Well, she has an *idiot* who is so in love with her, … and you can tell her so."

"With your permission I will, but don't you think ….."

"You're right. … I want to tell her myself, … show her ….."

"Look, you stopped trembling, Jonathan."

"Because I'm happy, … relieved, … and so grateful. Thank you. … Thank you. … Thank you."

"Jonathan, … I thank God that you're the man I thought you were."

(the next day Kathie and Ana talk …)

"How are you this bright cheerful morning? … Did you sleep well, Anastacia?"

"Kathie, … if you don't mind, … I don't feel well. I could use some more sleep."

"Not this morning, Dearee. I need to talk to you."

"Couldn't it wait until later … when I wake up?"

"I talked to Jonathan, Ana."

"What? … When? … How?"

"Wow. You bolted right up."

"Just tell me, Kathie. Tell me."

"Hold on, Ana. … Hold on."

"Sit here on the bed. … Well?!"

"Don't you want to sleep a little longer?"

"This is not funny. Talk! … Please, talk to me, Kathie."

"Well, … I hope that you won't be mad at me."

"I know. I already know that he's done with me, … but he talked with you? … Where did you run into him?"

"Well, it didn't quite happen that way."

"This isn't funny. Please don't play games with me. … I'm sick."

"Well, Ana, you're just going to have to get well."

"I mean it, Kathie."

"Come on. … Sit up. … It's all good news."

"What do you mean? … Did you talk to him or not?"

"Ana, you have it all wrong. … You think he doesn't care."

"I *know* he doesn't care. I tried many times to contact him. … He is purposely avoiding me."

"Ana, that *was* true, … but it was because you told him you no longer knew him."

"What? ... What are you talking about? ... I haven't seen or spoken to him since ....."

"Ana, he said he saw you at a restaurant in NY; ... and ... he found the courage to approach you, and ... you told him that you don't know him, ... and to please leave you alone. So he did."

"What? What kind of story are you telling me? I've never been to NY, and I have not spoken to him since ....."

"I know. I know. And I told him that, Ana."

"So, ... you have spoken with him."

"Yes. Yes. Get up, and I'll tell you the whole story."

"I should be mad at you for going behind my back. ... You know I love you, Kathie, ... but not as much as Jonathan. So, ... I have a *doppelganger* in NY?"

"It seems so. ... Hurry. Take a shower right now, Ana."

"I'm better already! ... I no longer feel sick. ... I guess the best medicine is mutual love."

(Kathie and Ana meet up with Jonathan ...)

"There he is, Ana. ... See, ... over in our old booth."

"I'm nervous, Kathie."

"Don't be. You look gorgeous. ... It's amazing how a couple of good days out of bed and the old beautiful you is back."

"Jonathan, don't get up."

"Don't be silly. ... I need a hug, Anastacia."

"Hey. Cool it you guys. No kissing. ... Get a room."

"Ok. Ok. ... Sit over there."

"Well, ... it seems that we have a lot to talk about ... so let's ....."

"Hey, Kathie, Jonathan wants us to leave. He's a little embarrassed about tearing up."

"It's ok. Just go. I know you want to be alone. ... I get it."

(the next morning …)

"Well, Ana?"

"Well, … what?"

"Come on. Come on."

"Well, Kathie, it was just the best day of my life. … He loves me. … He truly loves me. … We just cried in each other's arms. He couldn't talk. He really was choked up; … but he put his hands around my face, and looked into my eyes with his dripping eyes, and he spoke to me with those beautiful blue tear-filled eyes, and I heard and felt everything. … I have never been so in love. He showered me with a passion, slow and deliberate. … Without one spoken word, he told me how much he loved me."

"Wow."

"Yeah. … That's how I feel."

"Well, the way you told that story, I thought I was listening to a romantic novel."

"It's amazing. Just amazing. Yesterday I wanted to die and now ….."

"Oh Ana, ... don't cry. Come here."

"I'm just so happy. ... I know I shouldn't be crying, ... but I can't help it, Kathie."

"Oh, Babe, these are happy tears. They're just washing away all the bad that you have been going through."

"What would I do without you, Kathie? ... You truly are my best friend."

"And don't you forget it! ... But now you need to clean up. Go. ... Do your thing. I want to see my gorgeous, beautiful friend back into the world of the living."

"I love you, Kathie."

"I love you too, Ana. ... Go. Now, go!"

(the next day ...)

"How do I look, Kathie?"

"You're back, ... but you could put on a couple of pounds, Ana."

"Yeah, ... I thought the same thing. A little skinny, though."

"Just a little, ... but you still have the curves and everyone is jealous of those."

"Yes, ... I know. I used to hunch over, so no one would notice."

"Babe, people pay big bucks to have big fake ones. ... You stand erect and be proud, Ana."

"You know, ... I need to talk to someone. ... Can I talk to you?"

"What a silly question. Come over here. Sit down. What's up, Ana?"

"What am I going to do when he finds out?"

"Who knows how he will react. He's so moral. He is also in love with you. He is probably more in love with you than you are with him."

"No. No. Not possible. I'm over the hill. ... I couldn't possibly love him any more than I do. He is so handsome. He is perfect. He touches me and I quiver. ... We make love and every thing he does is perfect, … perfect, … perfect. I don't think I could be more in love."

"Yeah, … I get it. … He's perfect."

"I'm sorry. I know I'm being silly, … but what a difference a day makes."

"I'm the one who is glad, Ana. … I was really worried about you."

"But I'm so confused. … Happy, but scared."

"Listen, Dear, I'm going to make an appointment with Dr. Mesmer for you. … He is the best therapist around. … I've heard he has done miracles with people. He could be more than helpful."

"Do you think I really ….."

"Yes. … Yes, I do. Everyone could benefit from good counsel. And he is the very best."

SECTION FOUR

THERAPY

ANASTACIA AND DR. MESMER

"Please. Show yourself into my office. I'll be with you shortly. ……. Well, first off, how shall I address you?"

"My name is Anastacia Romanov, … but I prefer you just call me *Ana*; … and I will address you as *Dr. Mesmer*. … Does that sound ok with you?"

"Sounds perfectly respectful to me. … So, … shall we begin?"

"I'm ready, Dr. Mesmer."

"Well, Ana, I've heard a lot about you. As you are probably quite aware, your father and I go way back to our Harvard years."

"Yes, so I understand. … You were roommates or something?"

"Actually, we were fraternity brothers."

"I've heard a lot of stories about *the society*, or something like that. What's that all about?"

"Well, Young Lady, … that … is something I am not at liberty to discuss with you."

"Doctor, … I'm hoping we can get around that … because … I need answers from you."

"Well, I can see that this is way more complicated than I had realized. … There could be a conflict of interest here. … I think I should refer you to a very competent therapist I know of."

"Dr. Mesmer, please. … I need your help. Only you four doctors know the story I need to hear."

"I think you're referring to the doctors I graduated with from Harvard?"

"Yes. … The four of you all work here at Superior General."

"Ana, you *are* aware that there were many more graduates than just us four."

"Yes, I hired a detective agency and I have obtained extensive files on everyone."

"Why would you do that?"

"Because I need to know something, Dr. Mesmer."

"And what might that be?"

"First, are you willing to take me on?"

"Well, … this is not how I expected our first encounter to go. I am going to have to ponder this."

"Are you going to confer with your frat brothers about me?"

"Possibly. This could concern them."

"But, don't you have a confidentiality agreement with me?"

"Ana, you're making this situation very difficult."

"Dr. Mesmer, … please. … I don't mean to be obstinate, but I desperately need your help."

"I'll get back to you in a few days. … I need to think this through."

"Please, … please, … please, Dr. Mesmer. … I'm begging you. … Can you assure me our conversation will go no further?"

"I'm an honorable man. … Also, … it would be unethical. So … yes, I promise."

(A few days later, Dr. Mesmer makes a decision …)

"Ana, I've debated this back and forth, and *do* believe me; … I almost backed out of doing this."

"Does this mean you will help me, Dr. Mesmer?"

"This means I will *try* … to help you."

"Thank you, Dr. Mesmer. … This means so much to me. So, … how does this work?"

"It's simple. … You talk. … I listen."

"No. No. NO. … I need answers. … I need conversation."

"That is *not* how it works, Ana."

"I know that this is not normal. I know that. But … I am asking, … begging, … pleading with you. Will you give it a try, Doctor?"

"You're making this very uncomfortable. … But I will try. … Be at my office Thursday, ten o'clock sharp. That's my day off. I'll set aside three hours."

(Thursday …)

"I see you're here a little early, Ana."

"Dr. Mesmer, … I'm so anxious to get started I barely got any sleep."

"Ok, then. Let's get started. … What is your story?"

"Well, Doctor, … what I tell you may shock you."

"I doubt that. I have heard it all, as they say."

"Ok then. … Here goes. … I'm having my *brother's* child. … Are you shocked?"

"Not yet."

"How about my dad is not my father."

"Interesting, since I know your dad personally. …"

"Hey. … Dr. Mesmer, I want to express my gratitude right away."

"About what, Ana?"

"You're talking to me. … We're conversing."

"This is different. ... Very different, ... and I am trying. How about explaining in a little more detail what you're looking to learn."

"Ok. ... Well first, I know that you and Dad attended Harvard together. Right?"

"Yes, that's correct. We were frat mates, and we traveled in the same social circles. ... We shared some good times together."

"Oh. ... Thank you again. ... This is wonderful. We're conversing very well."

"Yes, ... but there is some personal stuff your dad would not appreciate my divulging."

"You just tell me what you feel comfortable telling me, ... ok?"

"Fair enough. ... So, ... why do you believe your dad is not your *biological* father, Ana?"

"It's a long story."

"Ok. ... Let's hear it."

"Well, ... it all started when I was very young. I overheard my mother and her twin sister, my aunt, whispering very secretly to each other; ... and I wanted to know why I couldn't be in on the secret. ... Because I was too *young* was the answer."

"So, ... did you find out the secret?"

"Yes I did."

"And ... ?"

"And one of the doctors from Harvard is my ... *biological* ... father."

"And how did you come to this conclusion, Ana?"

"First, Doctor, let me ask you some questions. Ok?"

"Ok."

"What do you remember about the high IQ Mensa program?"

"Yes. ... I remember that program very well."

"I'm listening."

"It was a big deal at the time. Very prestigious to become a member. ... To qualify, you had to have a very high IQ and pass a very rigorous testing regime."

"How did that go?"

"That's how we all met each other. We bonded over that program."

"I have some more questions, Doctor."

"What are they?"

"What do you know about the Mensa Sperm Donor Program?"

"Now *that* may be getting too personal."

"It's important. ... Very important. ... Please. ... Tell me what you know."

"They came around to all the members, ... men and women, ... and looked for willing members to be part of the program. ... I personally did not participate in that program; ...but , ...as I recall, everyone else in my circle did."

"Why didn't you participate?"

"That is personal, ... but ... I will answer the question. The woman I married adamantly did not want children, ... so ... I had a vasectomy."

"Thank you, Doctor, for your honesty."

"What else can I help you with, Ana?"

"Now, … do you get the picture? … I am the product of that Mensa Sperm Donor Program."

"So … that's the secret, … is it?"

"And, … my boyfriend also is."

"And that's how you came to the conclusion that your boyfriend could also be your *brother?*"

"You got it."

"Ok, ok. … It's starting to make some sense here."

"So, … what can you tell me, Dr. Mesmer?"

"I have to be careful what I say, … what I divulge to you."

"Please. … Just be honest. … Did you know my mother and her twin sister, … my aunt?"

"What are their names?"

"My mother's name is Marina and my aunt's name is Anastacia, … the same as mine. I was named after her."

"I *do* remember them."

"Is that all you can tell me?"

"They were both very very beautiful women."

"What were they like back then? ... I need more information."

"They were very popular; ... and ... as I recall, very involved in that sperm donor program as recruiters."

"Anything else?"

"I am curious, Ana; and as I recall it, ...they just seemed to disappear one day. They dropped out of Harvard and couldn't be found."

"Yes. My mother dropped out of college to marry my dad, and my aunt married that rich tycoon. As I later learned, he didn't want children; and she agreed to his terms. But, ... he was very good to her in every other way. She wanted for nothing."

"I always wondered what happened to them. Like I said, ... they just disappeared, ... vanished, ... gone, ... no trace of them."

"You seem disturbed, Dr. Mesmer. ... So, ... you *did* know them?"

"Yes. Yes I did. ... So, let's continue with your story, shall we?"

"What can you tell me about Dr. David Danner?"

"He is the head of Superior General. He is a very driven man, ... a no-nonsense kind of man, ... a strong-willed kind of man."

"Well, ... then he is a possibility?"

"Yes, yes. He was a sperm donor."

"Do you know Jonathon Masters, my boyfriend?"

"Yes. ... A very handsome young man, ... very intelligent. ... He is also just like Dr. Danner, graduated in the number one spot at Harvard."

"I am aware of that. ... What else do you know?"

"Dr. Danner competed all through our college years with Jonathan's father. ... That is why Jonathan had to be number one in his graduating class to ... please his father."

"Well, ... it seems that his dad confessed to Jonathan that he is ... NOT ... his *biological* father."

"So, … you're saying that it's possible that Dr. Danner is the sperm donor for both you *and* Jonathan?"

"That, sir, is the possibility. … Yes. YES."

"Quite intriguing. … And, … that's how you came to think you might be brother and sister?"

"When Jonathan came to this conclusion, … he wanted nothing to do with me."

"I take it he is a religious man?"

"More like a very moral man."

"And what do you think of all this, Ana?"

"I love him. … I just love him. … I think I love him *too* much."

"It takes time, … and … time is the healer. … Trust me. … You will get over him."

"No. No, Dr. Mesmer, I won't."

"Why do you question me?"

"Because you still don't know all the facts here."

"Enlighten me."

"I'm having his baby."

"Well, … yes. … That does alter things a bit, doesn't it?"

"And, Doctor, please don't offend me by suggesting ….."

"No, I won't. I can tell that is out of the question for you. Does he know?"

"I was getting very sick and confused, and I contemplated some very bad things."

"Tell me what happened, Ana."

"My best friend, Kathie, found me out. She took away my pills and hid them or flushed them. It was very close. I was really at my rope's end."

"I understand. … I understand that this is very hard to talk about. … Just try to calm down there. Just relax a little. … Wipe away those tears. … We're making some very good progress here. I am with you all the way now."

"Oh, thank you, Dr. Mesmer. … Thank you. … I am so so grateful you understand."

"That's better. ... Much much better. ... I'm starting to understand the big picture here. ... I have never dealt with a case that I was a part of, ... so ... I have to approach this as unchartered territory."

"I understand. ... I totally understand, Doctor; ... and I profusely thank you. I know that you're going way out of your normal boundaries, and I am so so grateful to you."

"Well, Young Lady, ... I somehow can tell that you are a very special person; and I very much belong in your corner."

"Oh, Dr. Mesmer, it means so much to hear that from you. I feel so much better now. You have given me hope."

"Trust me. I feel that the pieces are coming together. I am starting to understand what is going on here. I would like to get Jonathan involved. Would he cooperate?"

"We have been open and honest with each other. He knows I am seeing you. I am sure he will be on board."

JONATHAN AND DR. MESMER

"Jonathan, Ana and I appreciate your involvement in her therapy sessions."

"As I'm sure you're aware, Dr. Mesmer, I'm very much in love with that lady; and anything I can do to help her, I'm very happy to do."

"Jonathan, as I'm sure *you're* aware, Ana has expressed mutual feelings for you. … Well, … let's get to the problem at hand here. … Anastacia has briefed me on the situation. Let's hear your side … as you see it. And, by the way, … this is not going to be the standard therapist encounter. I promised Ana to be open and forthright."

"She truly appreciates that, Dr. Mesmer, and so do I."

"So, … let's start from the beginning. … How did you two meet, Jonathan?"

"Well, … as you know, she is relatively new at this hospital, as am I. I was having my lunch break, and … in walks this beautiful beautiful woman."

"So, … you *noticed* she was beautiful … right?"

"You're funny, Doctor."

"Just trying to lighten this up a bit. … So, how did you finally meet Ana?"

"I was advised that UTOPIA, where I reside, was recently purchased by Anastacia and Kathie; and I used the excuse of complimenting them on the new renovations."

"Very clever move on your part."

"Well, … her best friend noticed and thought we should meet."

"Well, Young Man, … they say you have *movie star good looks,* … which is a complement to you."

"Thanks for that compliment, Doctor, … but to get on with my story, … I really think it was love at first sight for me."

"Perfectly understandable. … And, so you obviously met?"

"Yes. Her friend set us up, and we instantly clicked. And, I guess that you should know that we were both virgins."

"You seem to have handled that problem very well on your own, Jonathan."

"Yes. We did alright with that one."

"It seems we have quite a love story going on here."

"More like a *Shakespearean tragedy*, don't you think?"

"Let's agree to think positive. I have a feeling … everything's going to work out … just fine."

"If Ana turns out to be my *sister*, I have no Idea how to react, Dr. Mesmer."

"I promise you, … we will get to the bottom of this. Will you trust me?"

"Doctor, to tell the truth, I have always met every challenge that has been thrown at me. But this one? … I don't know about."

"Will you trust me?"

"I'll try, Doctor."

"Jonathan, I am not telling you everything I have up my sleeve … until … I am sure."

"What do you mean by that remark?"

"You … just be positive and patient my boy, … ok?"

"Ok."

CONCLUSION

"What are we going to do, Jonathan?"

"What *should* we do, Ana?"

"All the paperwork is ok. ... Birth certificates, etc."

"Listen, I can't live without you. ... If you're my half-sister, so be it, Ana."

"I can't let you go against your morals, Jonathan. We can live together without, ... you know."

"Without any physical intimacy? ... Can *you* do it, Ana?"

"Yes. Yes, I can. ... I need to be with you. ... I love you."

"Let's do it then, Ana."

"Can I think about it, Jonathan?"

"No. I'm going to make the arrangements."

"Justice of the Peace?"

"No. A real wedding."

"But … a small wedding. … Ok?"

"Ok."

DR. MESMER AND JONATHAN
(THE REVEAL)

"How are you coming along with your project, Jonathan?"

"Lots of pieces here."

"Well, … I can see you're quite consumed."

"Can I talk to you about this? … I need your insight, Dr. Mesmer."

"Well, … I am just as intrigued by all this as you are. … So … where are you at?"

"Well, … Ana has a very secret detective agency here to help her, and that has given her some very secret information that could not be gotten elsewhere."

"This story is evolving into quite something else, … isn't it?"

"Yes, Doctor, … it certainly is."

"She had to sign secrecy contracts and everything. … She was not supposed to tell me, … but she did."

"So, … you're saying that she can get information from this agency … that … she can't get anywhere else?"

"Yes. … What do you make of that, Dr. Mesmer?"

"I don't know what to make of that."

"She was given a box that was supposed to be a clue of some sort to be opened on her 25th birthday … at … a lawyer's office."

"Well, … that's a little intriguing. … So, … what happened?"

"The story she told me was that she went; … and then at exactly four o'clock on her birthday, she met the lawyer. … He gave her a key. … She opened it, … and … NOTHING WAS INSIDE. … So that was a *dud*."

"What kind of box, Jonathan?"

"It was a carved box. … Well done. … Why do you ask?"

"I find that subject fascinating. ….. I have come to a conclusion. … Just curious. ….. Trying to help you put the puzzle together, Jonathan. ….. I would like to see that box sometime."

"I'll bring it the next time I come, Doctor. … I understand your interest in that."

"Yes. … I'm surprised that you know … that … I'm interested in that sort of thing."

"I did my research. ….. You investigate *paranormal* subjects."

"Talking about that subject, … what is your analysis of the lady, Jonathan?"

"I have become very fond of her. … A very strange bond is happening, and I'm very much involved; … but … Dr. Danner has signed me up for thoroughly debunking her,… so to speak."

"Dr. Danner …*IS* … very biased, … isn't he?"

"He is a no-nonsense sort of guy, … and … has a very strong opinion about this. … He wants all the rumors about the lady to stop. … He is very worried about the hospital's reputation."

"How are you going to handle it?"

"Well, … he wants me to prove that she is a fraud. … And … I have already witnessed and participated in *paranormal* events."

"I have also been assigned to work with the lady … after … you make your evaluation."

"Well, … I have a deal for you. … Since you're going to work with her after my evaluation, … I will give you my honest opinion of what I find … and … a watered down version … to appease Dr. Danner."

"I agree. … Dr. Danner is not going to accept … anything … but a debunking."

A LITTLE CHAT

"Jonathan, why are you looking so glum?"

"I'm sorry. I just have a lot on my mind lately, Ana."

"Can we have a little chat about this? ... A little huddle or a cuddle?"

"You're always so upbeat. I like that about you. I apologize for my moodiness."

"I think you should take a break from the lady, don't you think, Jonathan?"

"You always seem to know what I am thinking about."

"Well, you always seem to be thinking about the same thing ... the lady ... *correct*?"

"It's just that I can't quite figure out what is happening here, Ana. ... It's all very strange."

"What is *strange*, Jonathan?"

"I feel as if I know her ... *really* know her."

"Maybe she is just nice … compatible. Look how we just took to each other right away too."

"Maybe you're right, Ana. Yes, … you could be right. I liked that lady, … right away good feelings from the start; and I could tell she felt the same way about me."

"Well, that is certainly a good thing since you *are* her main doctor, *correct*?"

"Yes. Dr. Danner has been wanting me to evaluate her unusual abilities, Ana."

"That seems like it would be fun … and challenging at the same time."

"You're right about *challenging*."

KATHIE & ANA DISCUSS JONATHAN

"Kathie, … I can't tell you too much, but I think I am making progress."

"You're talking about Jonathan?"

"Of course. … I have nobody but him."

"Oh, … of course not, Ana. … The rest of us don't count, do we?"

"Come on. … You know what I mean. … Do you want to hear or not, Kathie?"

"Ok. … Let's hear it."

"Well, at first he would not say anything. … But I finally got him to open up a little, and now he is telling me things."

"What things?"

"I can't tell you."

"And … may I ask … *why* you can't tell me, Ana?"

"Because, … I can't betray him, … his trust."

"Then *why* are you talking to me?"

"Because you are my best friend, Kathie."

"Do you know how ridiculous you have become?"

"Ok. Ok. … It's because I don't want *you* to think he has lost it."

"Why would I think that?"

"Because, … I *am* worried … that … he has lost it."

"I am for real thinking that *you* have lost it, Ana. … I hope no one overhears this conversation."

"Why Kathie?"

"Read my mind."

"Wow. Wow. … I can't believe you just said that, Kathie."

"Ok. Ok. … This talk is crazy."

"No. No. … Listen to me. … Now I have to tell you. … I wasn't going to until you said *that*."

"Until I said what, Ana?"

"Until you said … *read my mind*. … That's what you just said."

"So?"

"So … that's what Jonathan and the lady are doing together."

"Explain, … please, Ana."

"They don't talk. … They read each other's minds."

"I don't believe you just told me that."

"Kathie, … you can't let on that you know."

"You're really serious, … aren't you?"

"Yes. Yes. This is for real. … Promise me, Kathie."

"Ok. Ok. … Quit shaking me. I promise. I promise. … But I still don't know what to make of this, Ana."

"I know. … Neither do I."

SECTION FIVE

SECRETS DISCOVERED

DR MESMER AND JONATHAN AND THE SPECIAL BOX

"Dr. Mesmer, ... thanks for seeing me on such short notice."

"You seemed to be in an anxious mood, Jonathan."

"I am. ... I am very concerned about Anastacia. ... She has regressed back into her depression."

"I had not heard about that."

"Well, ... I think it's about time we come clean about what is happening here, Doctor."

"What do you mean by that statement?"

"I have some pictures to show you."

"When did you take those pictures of my special box?"

"They ... are NOT pictures of ... YOUR box, Dr. Mesmer."

"Well, ... that *does* explain a lot doesn't it, Jonathan."

"Can you explain? ... Will you explain this to me?"

"I need to think about this. ... Please let's table this until I ponder over this."

"How much time do you need?"

"I will call you tomorrow, Jonathan. ... I promise."

(the next day ...)

"Jonathan, this is Dr. Mesmer. ... I am contacting you as I said I would. Please schedule an appointment as soon as possible."

(at the appointment ...)

"Thank you for your quick response, Dr. Mesmer."

"Jonathan, I apologize for not being forthright with my intentions. ... I was completely caught off guard by the revelations that were coming at me."

"Can you explain what you mean by that?"

"Yes. ... I will try with the best of my ability."

"I'm listening, Doctor."

"My special box … and Ana's box … were commissioned by me in honor of a relationship I had with the love of my life."

"Are we talking about Ana's *biological* mother?"

"I see you're getting the picture here."

"And I believe you're deciphering that you are the …..?"

"That seems to be the logical conclusion doesn't it, Jonathan."

"The next question is … why are the boxes empty, Dr. Mesmer?"

"They are *not* empty."

"That begs for an explanation."

"Let me show you. … Let's go to my box."

"Ok."

"Use the golden key and open the box, Jonathan."

"There is *nothing* inside."

"Use the little flashlight there on the stand and shine on the bottom. … What do you see?"

"I see what looks like a letter inscribed on the bottom panel, Doctor."

"That is a cherished letter to me from Ana's biological mother."

"That, Dr. Mesmer, solves the puzzle in more ways than one."

"And I think you will find that Ana's special box is not so empty either, Jonathan."

"I am sure she will be more than delighted to find that letter."

"I think today we found *more* than letters."

"And I am so grateful to have *lost* a sister!"

THE REGRESSION SESSION

"Jonathan, ... how are you feeling on this fine day?"

"A little anxious. ... A little nervous."

"Well, with your permission, ... we are going to take care of that."

"I have every confidence in you, Dr. Mesmer. ... Your reputation is *stellar*."

"Well, thank you my boy. ... All compliments are welcome here. I will do my best to live up to your expectations."

"How does this work? ... This is an area I know very little about."

"Well, let me explain this to you as I would to any new patient. ... You just relax there on my couch and get comfortable, Jonathan."

"This is a very comfortable couch."

"Yes. Nothing but the best for my patients. ... I have a patter I do with all my new patients. ... Just take in a big deep breath and hold it for two seconds. ... Now, slowly let it out and relax. … Deeply relax now. … Relax. … Relax, … like a rag doll, … loose, limp and relaxed. … Always follow my directions completely. We begin. … I am going to give you a complete explanation of what is going to happen here. … Is that agreed upon and acceptable with you, Jonathan?"

"Yes, I agree, Doctor. … Please treat me as you do any new patient. … I have very limited experience and would benefit from learning about hypnotism."

"Ok then. … I am going to give you the best tutoring I can. After all, you have, as my student, the direct descendant of the notorious Franz Anton Mesmer, … one of the earliest founders of hypnotism as we know it today."

"I am looking forward to your tutoring, Dr. Mesmer. … You know I love to learn."

"We begin…. There are four brain patterns that we are interested in. … They are described as BETA, ALPHA, THETA, and DELTA. … When we are engaged in heavy thinking, … fully alert, … we are operating in the BETA range. … We want to relax down into the ALPHA and even a lower brain wave, the THETA range. … This is where we do our best work. … So, … our first objective is to lower your brain wave, and also we want to produce a chemical called NITRIC OXIDE. … This can be produced by HUMMING and swallowing. … This will relax your nerve cells. ... Follow my instructions and we begin. ... Take a big, ... slow, ... deep breath and hum as you exhale. ... Another big, ... slow, ... deep breath and hum and swallow. ... And another, ... going deeper into this wonderful pleasant state of relaxed hypnosis. ... Very deep now. ... When I count backwards from ten to one, ... you will be in very deep hypnosis."

(... time passes ...)

"It is time to come up now. ... You will slowly come up. ... I will count from one to ten; and when I reach the count of ten, ... you will be fully awake, alert, and feeling wonderful."

(Dr. Mesmer counts slowly to ten ...)

"So, ... how was your experience, Jonathan?"

"Well, ... I don't know. ... I don't seem to remember anything, ... but I feel good. I feel *wonderful*."

"That is exactly what you're supposed to do. ... Excellent, my boy. ... I gave you a post hypnotic command to erase your memories of this session."

"Why would you do that?"

"It's to protect your mental well-being."

"Well, … Dr. Mesmer, I'm not sure I like that."

"Trust me, Jonathan. … I know what I am doing here."

"I am *NOT* comfortable with that. … You have this all recorded, … I assume?"

"Yes, … and it's all confidential and in safe keeping."

"I have to think about this."

ANA & JONATHAN DISCUSS REINCARNATION

"What happened with Dr. Mesmer, Jonathan?"

"I told you. … I got upset."

"You never get upset."

"What do you mean by that, Ana?"

"You're different. … I feel like I don't even know you anymore. … We have to talk."

"What do you want to know?"

"Everything, Jonathan. … If we're going to be partners, … I need to know what's going on here."

"If you really want to know, … it's crazy. … I feel like I'm losing it, Ana."

"You're acting like you're losing it. … You need to confide in me. … Can you do that? … Please."

"Do we really have to talk about this? … Ok. … Ok. I will, … but I don't think you can understand … because … I don't understand."

"Please, Jonathan, … just try. … I love you. … Make me understand."

"Ok. … Let me calm down. … You sit over there. I'll sit here. … Give me five minutes."

(Silence, as some time passes …)

"Jonathan, … how are you feeling?"

"Better. … Much better, Ana. … I'm calm now. … I'm contemplating what I should tell you."

"Let's not go there. … You already promised. … I'm listening."

"Well, … I'll start from the beginning. … Do you remember that Dr. Danner assigned that so-called strange lady to my care?"

"Yes. … She certainly has a reputation, doesn't she?"

"Believe me, … it's well deserved, … but just not what the reality is."

"This story is going to be interesting, isn't it?"

"That's an understatement, Ana. ... What I have experienced with her has me questioning everything."

"You seem to get upset very ... easily when you talk about her."

"Ok. ... I'll take a few deep breaths."

"Feel better?"

"Yes. ... Much better."

"Ok, Jonathan. ... I'm listening."

"Ok. ... Here goes. ... I need to ask you a question first, Ana."

"And ... what is that, Jonathan?"

"What do you know about *reincarnation*?"

"Not much. ... Just that some Asian societies take *that* seriously. ... Am I right about that?"

"You're right about that, ... but ... in our culture it is a fringe belief."

"What do you think about that, Jonathan?"

"That's where I'm going with this story. … I have never given much credibility to any religion. I have considered myself to be … agnostic."

"Does that mean you don't believe in anything?"

"Not really. … We're taught to think scientifically."

"You mean like our stern leader of the hospital, … Dr. Danner?"

"Exactly. … Dr Danner has the quintessential no-nonsense approach to everything, … and he expects his colleagues to think like he does."

"How does this relate to *your* story, Jonathan?"

"Before I met the lady, … I had heard all the stories."

"You mean all the crazy stories about her psychic abilities?"

"Yes. … All that … and more, … and Dr. Danner is relying on me to give him a detailed report debunking the whole thing."

"Then, … why don't you?"

"Because I'm ethical. … I'm not going to make up what I think he wants to hear … if … it's not true."

"Are the stories true then?"

"I don't know. … That's what is confusing. … I have to question what I am experiencing with her."

"I can see now why you're upset. … You feel an obligation to do the right thing, … don't you?"

"There is more to this story … that I have not told you yet, Ana."

"Jonathan, … I think you need to let everything out. … You need to have someone you trust on your side … and I hope it's me. … Do you trust me?"

"It's not that I don't trust you. … I'm embarrassed about my thought processes, … and I don't want to lose your respect for me."

"Jonathan, … you could never stop my respect for you. I hope you feel that you can trust me enough to tell me everything."

"I have had some extraordinarily deep conversations with this lady, … and … I have been holding back divulging the depth and meaning behind those conversations."

"Can you tell me about that?"

"I have been working with her for many months now … and … have followed her progression from not knowing who she was to slowly evolving into this *extraordinary* lady. … And I mean *truly* extraordinary. … Beyond belief, Ana."

"I'm listening, … and … you're making me understand what you're going through."

"Do you believe in destiny?"

"Why do you ask that?"

"Do you think things happen for a reason, Ana?"

"I don't know how to answer that question."

"Neither do I … Now, do you get it?"

ANASTACIA'S DIARY

Dear Diary .....

What to make of this? ... His story sounds crazy. ... Oh. ... Oh. ... I feel so bad for him. ... I love Jonathan so much. ... Am I helping or hindering? ... He needs answers ... by himself. ... He even said so. ... Ok. ... Ok. ... I'll just be there when he needs me.

WHAT'S BOTHERING YOU?

"What is bothering you, Jonathan? You're in such deep thought."

"Ana, if you only knew what I am experiencing."

"You have said that many times, and still I don't understand; and that worries me. Can't you try to explain it to me?"

"I'm not sure I know *how* to explain it."

"It has something to do with your session with Dr. Mesmer, doesn't it?"

"You're pretty intuitive to figure that out, Ana."

"You're upset with Dr. Mesmer, aren't you?"

"He seems to be holding back information that I want to know."

"Can you explain how he is able to do something like that?"

"I have agreed to do more hypnosis sessions with him."

"And just what does that entail, Jonathan?"

"He has suggested that I have *somnambulistic traits*."

"And what does that mean?"

"That means I go very fast and very deep into the *trance state*."

"Is that good or bad?"

"It could be good. ... *Very* good, ... *IF* he would share his findings with me, Ana."

"And why isn't he? ... I assume that is your concern."

"That is very much my concern. I want to know. I believe I *should* know, ... but ... for some reason Dr. Mesmer feels he is protecting me."

"That does seem irrational that he would withhold anything from you. ... What are you going to do?"

"That's why you found me in deep thought. I haven't figured *that* out yet, Ana."

"Another puzzle, huh, Jonathan."

DR PHENOM DISCUSSES JONATHAN WITH DR MESMER

"Dr. Phenom, it has been a while hasn't it?"

"Well, Dr. Mesmer, you certainly haven't changed much, … still the handsome dude we all were jealous of."

"And I can see you're still master of the glib talk."

"My understanding is you're in need of advice concerning your interaction with our boy Jonathan Masters."

"I have some very challenging circumstances that could benefit from your counsel, Dr. Phenom."

"You're talking about the lady they are addressing as Angela?"

"Yes. It seems to very much concern the lady and her interaction with Jonathan."

"Well, she *is* quite a *phenomenon*, isn't she."

"And that is why I am calling on my esteemed colleague Dr. Phenom to address this *phenomenon*."

"Ha. Ha..Enough of this, Dr. Mesmer. Let's be serious. What is of concern here?"

"Well, I have initiated some rather extensive *hypnosis* sessions with Jonathan."

"And what are the results?"

"Rather astounding, to be blunt, Dr. Phenom."

"Please elaborate. I'm intently listening."

"Where to begin … I'll start with I have blocked his retention of all memories of our sessions."

"How is he reacting to that? … And *why* would you do that, Dr. Mesmer?"

"To answer that, I have to explain my reasoning …"

"Yes. Please do, as I cannot fathom any reason for withholding information from a patient."

"Let me start by explaining why revealing *that* information could be detrimental to Jonathan."

"I'm listening *intently*, Doctor."

"Jonathan has expressed to me how he has been questioning his take on reality."

"That seems like an odd thing to say."

"Not really, Dr. Phenom, when you hear his stories about his experiences with the lady."

"That sounds like a very intriguing story line."

"Believe me it *is*. He was very reluctant to reveal his experience with the lady."

"I am anxious to hear *that* story, Dr. Mesmer."

"Dr. Phenom, I have to ask you some personal questions first."

"Why is that?"

"Because it is important. … Bear with me here."

"What is it you want to know?"

"I believe that you are a very religious man. Am I correct?"

"Yes. I have no qualms about expressing that to anybody … I am a firm true *believer*."

"That is what has been told to me, ... and that is why I asked for your visit to me, Dr. Phenom."

"Why is that so important, Dr. Mesmer?"

"I'll get to that. Please bear with me here. ... I understand that you teach a Bible study. Am I correct on that?"

"Yes. I teach at my church on Fridays and Sundays."

"So I take it that you're very well rehearsed with the Bible ... correct?"

"Where are you going with this questioning?"

"I am asking you to just answer some questions. Please, again, bear with me, Dr. Phenom."

"Ok. Ok. Ask away."

"Who is John ... in Bible times?"

"Well, there are a couple John's that come to mind: one was a disciple of Jesus and wrote five of the books in the Bible; ... and another was John the Baptist, a relative of Jesus' and whose primary role was to prepare the way for the coming of the Lord."

"*That* is what I needed to confirm."

"So, how is this relevant?"

"I have been doing *regression therapy* with Jonathan, and we have entered Biblical times."

"So, are you saying what I think you're saying, Dr. Mesmer?"

"Dr. Phenom, now you see why it is important that Jonathan doesn't have to deal with this knowledge at this time."

"Yes. Yes. I can see why you must traverse slowly here; and, as a *believer* myself, I have a lot to ponder myself."

"Dr. Phenom, I know I don't have to tell you, ... this is all very confidential. Do I have your word on that?"

"Of course you do. I understand completely. I am very much in awe of this revelation. I have some researching to do myself, Dr. Mesmer."

"I trust you will keep me informed of your findings."

"Of course, Dr. Mesmer. Of course."

THE REQUEST

(Dr. Phenom requests a very urgent meeting with Dr.Mesmer about Jonathan ...)

"Dr. Mesmer, I don't think you know the magnitude of what is transpiring here."

"Dr. Phenom, I realize you are an avid *believer*, and that could influence your perception of the situation."

"I really don't know how to get through to you. We may just be witnessing the beginning of *prophecy*."

"Like I said, I have to be ethical to my trade; and your asking to listen to my regression tapes with Jonathan would be a betrayal of my oath."

"Dr. Mesmer, I need to explore what those regression tapes are about. This could be significant for our destinies."

"I appreciate your vigor, Dr. Phenom, ... but ... I must at this time decline your request."

I AM TOO

"Jonathan, this has become an obsession with you; and this has me very worried."

"This is just the way I react, and I don't know any other way to explain it, Ana."

"What is it about this Dr. Phenom,… that you don't want to meet up with him?"

"I want to honor … NO … I *have* to honor our code between Dr. Mesmer and myself."

"Can you tell me what that all entails so I can better understand what is transpiring here?"

"I will try, Ana, … but keep in mind what I tell you … what I reveal to you ….."

"I know, Jonathan. It's a *secret society* thing. I know."

"Ana, I know we're together and we need to share. For the sake of our relationship, I will divulge some secret society information; but you, in turn, must honor the *code of silence*."

"Even with Kathie?"

"Yes, Ana. Even with Kathie."

"I understand, Jonathan, and I will abide by your wishes."

"First, you should know that the society is comprised of many factions. It is very broad and you have to have very high standing to be privileged to all facets."

"You're a member, correct?"

"Yes, Ana. I became a member at an early age."

"So, … how involved *are* you, Jonathan?"

"I am a member in good standing and I have limited access."

"So it's *really* a *very* secret society."

"Yes, … and it wields great power; … and I should tell you that I know about your special agency. *THEY* … are an integral part of the society, Ana."

"So you know that I became a member of the agency, Jonathan?"

"Yes. I was informed of that, ... *or* ... I would not be communicating with you like this."

"Wow. What a small world, huh, Jonathan?"

NEXT SESSION

"Dr. Mesmer, I am having a very difficult time accepting your policy of *not* revealing findings of our hypnosis session."

"Well Jonathan, there is a very valid explanation for withholding that information at this time."

"I would very much appreciate an explanation of why that is so."

"Jonathan, we have scheduled, as I recall it, six sessions. Am I correct on that?"

"What has that to do with *my* concerns, Dr. Mesmer!?"

"I'll explain … because any knowledge prematurely attained *could* and *would* influence the next sessions. … Jonathan, you have to trust me on this. I know what I am doing."

"I am trying not to be upset or concerned, but I find this approach unacceptable to me."

"Well, Jonathan, that certainly is your prerogative. With that, I believe our session is now over."

"Dr. Mesmer, what about the tape recordings?"

"I stand by my previous decision. Good day, Jonathan."

WHAT HAPPENED?

"Jonathan, you seem upset. What happened?"

"We terminated our session, Ana."

"Why would you do that?"

"Because I became upset … angry!"

"Angry? … You don't get angry, Jonathan."

"Well I did this time … and I don't like this feeling."

"Why don't you just go for a walk and calm down a little."

"Good idea. … Great idea. … I'll be back in a while. I apologize to you, Ana, and I'm truly sorry about my behavior here."

"No need for apologies, Jonathan. Go, go, go."

(Kathie overheard Ana's conversation …)

"Ana, I overheard your conversation with Jonathan. What is going on here?"

"Wow. I don't know, Kathie. I don't think I've ever seen him this upset."

"Something must have happened to get him this upset. Do you have any idea what could have caused this to happen?"

"Kathie, I think it has something to do with his sessions with Dr. Mesmer."

"Will he talk with you about it?"

"We will see. … We will see."

THE CALL

"Is this Ana?"

"Yes it is, Dr. Mesmer. I recognize your voice."

"Ana, I need to converse with Jonathan. Is he there?"

"No he is not, but I will see him later. Can I give him a message?"

"Ana, can you please relay to him that I suggest we should talk."

"I will relay that message to him, Dr. Mesmer. Thanks for calling."

(Later ...)

"Jonathan, you have a message asking you to call Dr. Mesmer."

"Ana, when did he call?"

"About two hours ago."

"Thanks."

"Well, what are you going to do?"

"What are you talking about?"

"Come on, Jonathan, ... how are you going to handle this?"

"I haven't had time to think this through yet, Ana."

"Do you want my advice?"

"Ok, let's hear it. What do you advise?"

"Well, Jonathan, you have unresolved issues and you're not doing very well with this."

"So you think I should …..?"

"Yes. Yes I do. You have nothing to lose … and your sanity to gain."

"So, do you think I have been a little out of whack here lately, Ana?"

"You be the judge, Jonathan. … You be the judge."

THE APOLOGY

"Dr. Mesmer, this is Jonathan. I believe apologies are in order here."

"Jonathan, no apologies are needed, … just good old patience and understanding. What are you suggesting here?"

"Dr. Mesmer, a fresh start is my recommendation."

"Jonathan, recommendation accepted. How about Friday at 2 o'clock?"

"I will attend with a fresh attitude in hand."

"Jonathan, I will await your arrival with high aspirations for success."

ON TIME

"Exactly 2 o'clock. Right on time, Jonathan."

"Again, Dr. Mesmer, I appreciate your acceptance of my apology."

"You, my boy, are dealing with some tough revelations; and we are going to be facing even tougher situations down the road. Please expect some turbulence. Together we will prevail. Are we in agreement, Jonathan?"

"We very much are, and I greatly appreciate your insights; but I have a question for you … who is Dr. Phenom?"

"Why? Has he contacted you?"

"Ana has informed me that he has tried to contact me several times, but I wanted to confer with you first."

"That was a wise decision on your part, Jonathan."

"Well, Dr. Mesmer, …*that* answer needs clarifying."

"I have been in consultation with Dr. Phenom about your unusual case, and I am sure you need details."

"You're right about that, Doctor."

"Dr. Phenom is a very unusual kind of doctor in that he relishes in the, shall we say, ... the *way out there* kind of cases."

"Well, that kind of describes *my* case, doesn't it?"

"That is why I consulted with Dr. Phenom in the first place; and you should know, he has had an encounter with Angela."

"That is interesting. Very interesting. And how did that encounter go?"

"Angela dismissed him."

"How does this all relate to me?"

"Dr. Phenom has a reputation of being very knowledgeable about aspects of your case that could be of great value to us."

"Can you elaborate?"

"Again, my boy, patience is of great value here."

"I am trying, Dr. Mesmer, ... BUT patience is not my thing."

A KITTY AT SUPERIOR GENERAL

"Ana, I couldn't wait to get home to tell you the cutest story about what happened at Superior General today."

"I already know … but let's hear *your* version, Kathie."

"How did you find out?"

"Jonathan told me his version, but let's hear what you have to say about that cute little kitty."

"*Cute little kitty* ? … I wouldn't call a 500 pound African lion a *cute little kitty*."

"I heard he was adorable and as sweet as any trained dog, Kathie."

"Well, the armed police were ready to put an end to any potential threat his escape posed to the public."

"*That* is where Jonathan's story begins."

"Ok. Ok. His version is probably much more interesting than us finding a beautiful African lion lounging on the hospital's lawn for all the world to see. … Top that story, Ana."

"Let's see what you think of the story Jonathan related to me."

"I'm listening."

"Well, it seems that Jonathan went for his scheduled session with the lady Angela; and when he entered the room, she was standing at the window with both hands directed at the beautiful African lion that was looking up at her."

"What was she doing?"

"She was saving his life by directing him to the hospital lawn and making him tranquil so he posed no threat to the public."

"She can do that, Ana?"

"According to Jonathan, she is one amazing lady."

"Well, I am very happy that the police did not have to resort to violence."

"Yes. The pretty kitty is safe at his home. Everything ended well."

"Thank goodness for that."

"Maybe we should thank *the lady*."

ANA'S GYPSY READING

"Ana, ... I hope you like walking around this renaissance fair as much as *I* do. ... When I saw it was in town again, I thought we could check it out *together*."

"Jonathan, I'm *really* liking this fair. ... The costumes are great; ... and ... I've *always* wanted to visit one of those Gypsy booths. ... You know, ... the ones with the *fortune tellers*."

"And *I* love the food ... and jousting demonstrations. ... Hey, Ana, ... there's one of those Gypsy booths. ... Why don't you give it a try. ... I'll meet you by the corn dog booth when you're done."

"Ok, Jonathan. ... Wish me luck."

(Ana goes into the Gypsy booth ...)

"May I ask your name? My name is Zara."

"My name is Anastacia Romanov."

"May I hold your hands, Ana ... I'm getting something here ... Your lineage traces back to the Russian Czar's children. Did you know that?"

"No, I was not aware of that."

"I believe that was on your mother's side, Anastacia. Also, I'm getting a link on your father's side to medieval medical practitioners … I'm drawn to France for some reason … something to do with hypnosis or something similar."

"Well, I find this very fascinating. I've always wondered about my lineage. This reading has certainly been interesting. I see my boyfriend is being impatient, so I've got to be going."

"Wait! There is more. Much much more coming through. Please don't go yet."

"I'm so sorry, but I have to go now. Bye."

(Ana discusses the Gypsy's reading with Jonathan …)

"Jonathan, do you think they do that with everybody?"

"What is that, Ana?"

"Make them feel they have an important lineage."

"Well, that is a rather good sales pitch, don't you think … to make you want to know more and come back for more of your story."

"That makes sense. Very rational thinking, Jonathan. It was all in good fun. I'm having a great time here at the fair with you."

"Could there actually be something to fortune telling?"

"Don't go there, Jonathan. Dr. Danner may be listening."

CURIOUS AND MYSTERIOUS

"Kathie, I have to tell you about something strange that happened to me on the way home yesterday."

"Didn't you go shopping for flowers at the garden center, Ana?"

"Yes, and it's right next door to where they're having that renaissance fair event."

"I thought you just attended that fair with Jonathan last week."

"Yes, we did; and I told you about our fortune teller experience."

"I remember. … You were not too impressed."

"Well, as I started to go by, I suddenly had this urge to go in."

"That's interesting, Ana."

"I followed my urge … right up to the fortune teller's booth."

"I'm listening."

"Kathie, I remembered that the fortune teller had urged me to come back, as there was more to tell me."

"I remember you saying that to me."

"Well, … there was a different lady this time."

"How was she different?"

"She was *old*, … and she wore old-time clothes."

"Old … and old-time clothes. Probably her costume for what she does, Ana."

"I don't mean to make fun, … but she could easily have jumped on her broom and flown away."

"Ha. Ha. That's funny. So, what happened next?"

"I remarked that I had been there before … and … had not finished my reading."

"So, what did she say?"

"She said, 'I know who you are.'"

"That was a strange thing to say, Ana."

"I thought so too, Kathie, as she was *not* there at the first visit … that I know of."

"Maybe she was in the back room listening … or something."

"Maybe, but that wasn't the strangest thing, Kathie."

"You have my attention. So … what happened next?"

"She beckoned me to sit down ... and … I did. She then looked at a row of what I assumed to be tarot cards. She was wondering which deck to use. She chose the OLD, … worn, … curled edge, … ancient-looking deck of cards."

"You're making this story of yours … mysterious, Ana."

"Because … IT WAS. Let me continue with what happened."

"You're a good story teller. I am intently listening."

"She handed me the deck. And said, 'shuffle.'"

"And?"

"And … I spilled the whole deck … onto the floor."

"What? … You did what, Ana?"

"Yes. … Yes. At first I jumped up … startled … and I started to bend over to pick up the cards. She shouted, 'No! Stop!!'"

"Ok. Ok. … Go on. … I'm listening."

"It gets stranger yet, Kathie."

"Come on. Tell the story."

"Well, … then she grabbed a large thin book and started fanning the pile of tarot cards spilled on the floor."

"Go on."

"And then, I observed that her fanning caused the cards on the floor … to form into a circle with ONE CARD in the middle."

"And … ?"

"And she told me to pick up the middle card, … NOT to look at it, … to hold it flat on my hand … and pass it to her."

"So … ?"

"So … I did as she told me to do, Kathie."

"And? … Finish the story."

"She just peeked at the card, … looked at me, … and slid the card back into the deck."

"Come on! … What was the card? … What meaning did it have? … She had to tell you, Ana."

"She motioned for me to GO. Her hand sweeping for me to GO. Just GO."

"You're kidding me. … You've got to be kidding me. You can't be serious."

"Well, at least she didn't charge me anything."

"That's how she left it? … That's all she said?"

"No. … That's not quite all she said. As I was leaving, she yelled after me, 'It's your boyfriend I want to see! Bring *him* back to me!!'"

TOO MUCH INFORMATION

"Ana, I have to ask … how does it feel to have found your father? Your *biological* father."

"Wow, Kathie. How did you know I was thinking about that?"

"It's very obvious that you're in deep thought about something."

"Well, you're certainly right about that."

"Do you want to share your thoughts with me?"

"I don't know how to answer that. I think I have to sort this out by myself."

"I can respect that, Ana."

"My emotions are all over the place."

"Well, this has been quite an emotional ride, hasn't it."

"Yes, Kathie. Yes it certainly has, and I'm so grateful that I *don't* have a brother."

"I agree. *Jonathan* just doesn't quite fit the bill as your brother."

"No. No. He doesn't. He's meant to be my love … my lover … my best friend … my everything."

"Here we go again."

"No. No. I'm sorry, Kathie. *You're* my best friend."

"I know. I'm just toying with you. I'm sorry; I shouldn't play with your emotions, as I don't really know what you're thinking."

"You and Jonathan are both the most important people in my life, and I am so grateful this has worked out this way."

"Ana! Ana! You're not thinking straight. There are more people coming in … and they're coming in fast."

"See. See how you do it. You bring me into reality. I have a new father, don't I?"

"*And* a new step mom."

"How do you think his wife is accepting all this?"

"Yes. Yes, can you imagine how *she* took all this in?"

"Yes, she certainly made it clear to him that she didn't want children. Remember, she insisted on a vasectomy."

"That made it pretty clear to him that she didn't want children in her life."

"I guess so. But what do you think will happen now, Ana?"

"Guess I'll find out soon, won't I?"

(Later ...)

"Ok. Ok. I need to know what happened, Ana."

"She made it very clear that she doesn't want to meet me."

"How do you know that?"

"It's simple. Dr. Mesmer told me so."

"You don't call him *Dad*?"

"No, I don't call him Dad."

"Why not? He *is* your father."

"My *biological* father ... *not* my Dad."

"Wow, Ana. Is that how it's going to be?"

"I'm confused. I don't know what to think. I'm grateful to find my *biological* father, BUT ….."

"But what, Ana?"

"Dr. Mesmer *is* my therapist."

"He is also your *biological* father."

"Don't you get it, Kathie? Who do I go to? … Who do I talk to? … I think I've lost my doctor."

"Ana, you certainly do have a lot to work out here."

"Don't worry, I'm just confused. I know how to work this out … I'll just talk to Jonathan. Jonathan will help me out."

"Great idea, Ana."

(Later with Jonathan …)

"Ana, of course you can talk to me, and you are showing signs of PTSD."

"I am so confused, Jonathan. So very confused."

"I can very well understand. What seems confusing, is normal."

"He doesn't know it *all*, does he?"

"Ana, what are you talking about?"

"Jonathan, does Dr. Mesmer know he has more children than just me?"

"Wow. Good question. I just remembered something. The psychic lady told Dr. Mesmer, at their first meeting, something that now finally makes sense."

"What are you talking about, Jonathan?"

"The way I heard it was he believed the psychic lady was not credible after their first meeting because she said he had *two beautiful daughters*. At that time, he believed he was childless because of his vasectomy."

"Do you think Dr. Mesmer remembers that conversation with that psychic lady?"

"I will find out if he remembers. I will ask him."

"Do you think that will be a little too much for him to take in right now, Jonathan?"

"He's a psychiatrist so he should be able to embrace this information."

"But will his *wife* embrace *two unwanted children*? Jonathan, this is a lot for *all* of us to absorb."

"We will just have to see how this is all going to play out."

"Drama. Drama. Lots of drama going on here."

"That's for sure, Ana."

(The next day ...)

"Ana, I was questioning how I should tell you this ….."

"Questioning what, Jonathan?"

"She left him."

"What! Because of me?!"

"Please don't go there, Ana. I was reluctant to inform you of this outcome."

"I won't bother them. I won't talk to her. She won't have to hear from me ever ever again, Jonathan!"

"Yep. Just as I expected. You're overreacting, Ana."

"No, I mean it. She won't have to worry about me interfering in their lives."

"Please. Please, just calm down. Stop crying."

"Why should I? She doesn't know me … she doesn't know anything about me."

"It will all work out like it should, Ana. I am here for you … and so is Kathie. We're all you really need."

"Jonathan, you're right. You and Kathie are all I really need."

"Always."

ADMIRATION

"So Jonathan, you have taken it upon yourself to be *my* therapist."

"With your permission, Dr. Mesmer."

"So you suggested there's something important I *need* to know, Jonathan?"

"Yes, I believe that you need to have all the information about what's transpiring."

"And what might that be, Jonathan?"

"Let me ask you a couple questions, Dr. Mesmer …"

"Shoot."

"Do you remember your first encounter with that psychic lady?"

"We're talking here about Angela, aren't we?"

"Yes, I believe that's what she's being called now, Doctor. And, as I recall it, your first encounter convinced you she was not credible because she stated you had *two* beautiful daughters."

"As I am now recalling it, I believe that's what transpired, Jonathan."

"Well, it seems that she is turning out to be *very credible*."

"So … my world really *is* being turned upside down. Are you telling me what I think you're telling me?"

"It seems so, Dr. Mesmer."

"How to take all this in …. Well … my wife just left me … one woman out … and I believe that you're telling me *two beautiful women* in."

"Well, Dr. Mesmer, you're still an amazing therapist aren't you."

"I *am* being challenged here, my boy. And I'm going to relish being your father-in-law."

"I stand by my admiration for you. So, please tell me *your* story, Dr. Mesmer."

JONATHAN AND DR. MESMER

"My father was very proud of being a direct descendant of the notorious Dr. Franz Anton Mesmer, ... the founder of *mesmerism*; ... but, for me, it was different. ... My father never went to university; and so he was very much intent on his offspring, ... which just unfortunately happened to be me, ... having the *duty* to carry on the glorious legacy."

"It's kind of obvious that you are not so happy about that, Dr. Mesmer."

"How would you like to be branded? ... *Franz Anton Mesmer, the 3rd* ? ... I had to memorize his birthday, ... May 23, 1734. ... And would you believe, ... May 23rd is *my* birthday too. ... My father thought that it was some kind of divine intervention; ... and as you can imagine, I have been burdened with my father's delusion of grandeur."

"We all have our cross to bear, don't we? ... I'm sure you have heard *my* story, haven't you?"

"Yes, Jonathan. I certainly have; ... and when I was told how you were pressured to be number one, just like Dr. Danner, ... I knew at that time I would sooner or later meet you. And I have greatly enjoyed our working relationship."

"You know, Dr. Mesmer, in all my studies, I have some extensive training in your field of psychiatry."

"Jonathan, I took the liberty to examine your credentials and degrees; and I would welcome you as a partner in my practice anytime."

"I consider that a great compliment. … I have a strange feeling that we are supposed to be right here at this time. … A little bit of déjà vu going here, I guess, Dr. Mesmer. Ha. Ha."

"Well, there is history going on here as I have spent a lot of hours in the company of your father watching and enjoying the competition between him and Dr. Danner."

"As I understand it, you were roommates?"

"We were more than that. We chose each other. We bunked together, and we enjoyed a lot of very deep conversations. When we decided to tackle the Mensa IQ challenge, your father outperformed everybody except Dr. Danner, Jonathan."

"Yes. … That became a big deal. Dad let me know, at an early age, that I was expected to excel."

"Well, … you certainly achieved that."

"I had to work extremely hard on that challenge; … but to be truthful, I really enjoyed that achievement."

THE (PRIVATE) NOTES

"Ana, did you notice that Jonathan left his private notepad right out there in the open?"

"He has always been so protective of his notes. Kathie, I think he did that on purpose."

"For what possible reason?"

"So we would find it and figure out what he is going through."

"Well, *that* is a little stretch, don't you think. Do you really think we should read them?"

"I'm sure. I'm sure. What do you make of this!? It's a handwritten note from those Gypsy people. I saw her give something to Jonathan at the fair."

"What does it say, Ana? Read it to me."

"It says, 'The pieces to a great and mysterious puzzle are being placed around you … not necessarily in front of you … You may choose to always be on the lookout … to the side, to the back, and front.'"

"Kathie, what the heck does all that mean to *you*?!"

(Jonathan comes in ...)

"Oh Jonathan! I hope you don't mind us reading your notes."

"It's Ok. It's all Ok."

"What does this mean, Jonathan?"

"That means exactly that ... the greatest puzzle I will ever face is being presented to me piece by piece."

"Jonathan, that is way beyond what I can assimilate."

"You asked for an explanation, and that is the closest I can come up with for an explanation by leaving you to find my notes."

"Thank you, Jonathan. Thank you for trying. I can see now ... no *try* to see ... try to be there for you ... even though this is way way beyond my comprehension."

"I want to thank both you girls for trying to be there for me."

"Well, I'm exhausted. This is all a little too much. I think I'll be leaving now."

"Thanks Kathie."

"Well, Jonathan, you've explained enough to me. I think I can understand. I can only … if you let me … go on this wild journey with you."

"Destiny is part of this puzzle, Ana; and everything is unfolding as it should."

"Jonathan, am I a piece of your puzzle? … Your destiny?"

"Anastacia, I believe you really are. I have learned that choosing the right path is always comfortable."

"Jonathan, am I comfortable?"

"Ana, you are very very comfortable."

"Jonathan, that is so comforting to me."

ANASTACIA'S DIARY

Dear Diary …..

*I write to talk of my perfect person who is not so perfect … a little moody … a little jealous … a lot conflicted … a lot too handsome … a lot too complicated. …..
Yes, Dear Diary, … not so perfect
….. Just perfect for me.*

SECTION SIX

COMMUNICATING

COMMUNICATING

"Jonathan, I very much enjoy our way of communicating."

"Angela, I think we have gone way beyond the doctor-patient status, haven't we?"

"That we certainly have. You may not fully comprehend the magnitude of what is transpiring here, but you should know that your input was vital."

"Angela, I'm not sure who has gained the most insight. I have been intellectually challenged by all that has transpired here."

"You're a very bright young man. ... You know how you like to deal with puzzles, ... well, the pieces are on the table so to speak; and I believe they are coming together rather nicely."

"Angela, I am so baffled by how you have taken on this witty, charismatic, playful attitude in your personality."

"Well, Jonathan, as they say, 'When in Rome, do as the Romans do.'"

"Ha. Ha. That's funny. It just seems that you adjusted to be so *normal*."

"Now that I am finally all manifested, so to speak, I am *normal* for *your* time."

"Your personality has blossomed dramatically since our first encounter, Angela."

"This may not immediately make sense to you, Jonathan, but know that fate has led the two of us to have the interaction we are experiencing."

"Sometimes … this seems like a dream."

"I can fully understand from your perspective, BUT … this is important … There is an instructional book I would like you to master."

"This book on meditation and dreaming?"

"Yes. I would like to *ring you up* now and then."

"I would like that, Angela."

"Jonathan, you have a very interesting life ahead of you."

SO BE IT ORDERED

"As the Exalted Commandant of this chapter, I have ordered a meet up of the ranking officers to address a pending challenge to our order of credibility. We have, it seems, in our midst a so-called supernatural being in the disguise of an entity called the PSYCHIC LADY. I hereby decree an Order of Investigation to be initiated to address the merits of this invasion of our perspective of reality. So be it ordered."

Exalted Commandant of Society

REAL NAME

"Have you experienced any strange or other unexplained events around our patient Angela?"

"Well, yes Dr. Mesmer, … I have. … I have wondered about something that transpired on the night shift."

"Let's hear it, Nurse."

"Well, we call the lady *Angela* because we don't know her real name; … Isn't that correct?"

"Yes."

"Well, I was working last Friday evening … and I was trying to locate Nurse Mary Perkins. … I thought I saw her enter Angela's room."

"Ok."

"So, … I went to the room and called in … asking, 'Mary, are you in here?' … And … I immediately heard the reply, 'Yes, I am here.'"

"So?"

"So, … it was … *Angela* that replied."

"Yes, … so … could her real name be … *MARY?* ….. You could have stumbled on something important here."

THE LADY'S EXPLANATION

"It took time for me to be all here."

"I'm sure there is an explanation for what you just said."

"Let's put it this way, … sometimes things work out just for His amusement. … You enjoy puzzles; … work it out."

"You certainly are a fascinating lady."

"Well, Jonathan, … on a more serious note, … I wish to thank you for all your patience with me and my finding myself and my purpose."

"What does that mean, Angela?"

"I will soon be departing as my destiny awaits my presence."

"You're being mysterious with me. … I don't see anything in your chart about your leaving us."

"Let's just say there is a much much larger chart that I follow. … Something like that famous quote from Shakespeare, … 'All the world's a stage, … and all the men and women are merely players.'"

"You are the biggest puzzle I have ever encountered, Angela."

"You have a very interesting life ahead of you, Jonathan; … and your place is to live it fully. …. And by the way, … I remembered my first name."

"Well, … *that* is a breakthrough. … What is it?"

"Ask the night nurse. … She called out my name, and I answered to it."

"More pieces of the puzzle?"

"Of course. … Life should be interesting. … See you in your dreams, Jonathan."

SOMETHING FOR ME

"Ana, I would like you to do something for me."

"What can I do for you, Jonathan?"

"I remember you telling me that you can receive any information that you could possibly desire from the special agency you belong to."

"What information are you looking to get?"

"I want to know all about this Dr. Phenom guy who is trying to make contact with me."

"How soon do you need this information, Jonathan?"

"As soon as possible."

"Consider it done."

(a few days later ...)

"Jonathan, this is very interesting. I hope you don't mind me reading about this Dr. Phenom guy."

"Well, your agency really *does* come through, don't they Ana. ... Please read away and bring me updates on this Dr. Phenom."

"So far it's very interesting. He has a lot of case files. ... What are *these* about? ... There are all kinds of titles ... Lucid Dreaming, Trance States, Hypnosis, Mesmerism, Possession, Voodoo Hallucination, Past Life Regression, Exorcism, ..."

"Stop right there, Ana!"

"Where? Past Life Regression?"

"Yes. Please pull all you can find on *Past Life Regression*."

"There is quite a bit here, Jonathan."

"Do you really want to get involved in all this, Ana?"

"Sure. If it can help, I am totally on board, Jonathan."

"Ok then. ... You take one half of these files and read them. I will do the same, and we can share our findings."

"Sounds like this could be fun."

"Ana, all of this is a gigantic puzzle that just needs to be put together."

"Jonathan, you know how you like a good puzzle."

"Well there certainly are a lot of pieces with this puzzle, Ana."

"First we have to find all the pieces."

"I think we're off to a good start."

"Ok. We're off!"

INTERESTING

"Jonathan, this Dr. Phenom is a pretty interesting man."

"Yes, Ana, I certainly agree that he has been involved in a lot of controversial areas, hasn't he."

"This is very fascinating reading, isn't it. What is *Lucid Dreaming*, Jonathan?"

"*That* is a fascinating subject. I know a classmate in college that was very much into it, and he would try to get me to experience it."

"Did you do it?"

"No. I was always too busy studying, … but that reminds me of something that my controversial patient Angela said to me …"

"That special patient of yours is causing quite a stir in your psyche, isn't she Jonathan."

"Angela is, as you put it, a *very special* patient."

"Is there a connection with your wanting all of this information on Dr. Phenom?"

"Ana, you are very intuitive. You are very much reading my mind."

"Ha. Ha. You're trying to be funny here, aren't you. That is what you supposedly do with the lady, isn't it Jonathan?"

"I am trying to make light of a serious situation. … Am I just *hallucinating* all of this … or … is something *supernatural* happening here?"

"Wow. So *this* is what this is all about."

"Yes, … and this is important to me."

COMMUNICATION

"Jonathan, how was your last session with your *special* patient?"

"Ana, do you believe in *Fate* and that things happen for a reason?"

"I don't know how to answer that. … Why do you ask *that*?"

"Do you remember yesterday talking about *lucid dreaming*?"

"Yes, Jonathan, and I have really dug deep into Dr. Phenom's files; and I have learned a lot. He has a tutorial … and I want to do it."

"Fascinating. Just fascinating. I am in awe of how this is all just coming together, Ana."

"What are you talking about? *What* is fascinating?"

"*Your* wanting to do *lucid dreaming,* Ana."

"So … ?"

"So … *that* is what the lady Angela wants *me* to do, … to become proficient at it."

"So you somehow think this is how *Fate* has ordained it, Jonathan?"

"That is eloquently put, … but yes. Yes I do, Ana."

"Why do you think the lady wants you to do this?"

"Communication."

"*Communication*, Jonathan?"

"Yes. She will be leaving shortly."

SHE'S GONE

"What happened?"

"*SHE'S GONE.*"

"What do you mean, ... *she's gone*? ... Who checked her out?"

"No one."

"What are you saying?"

"I'm saying ... that ... she *disappeared*. ... She just disappeared."

"That *can't* be so. ... Someone *had* to check her out. ... That's the procedure. ... How could this happen? ... You can't leave without going past the check out station. ... Did you ask security?"

"Of course. ... Everyone is searching around trying to find out what happened. ... They checked the security cameras, and ... so far *nothing*. ... This is strange. ... *Very* strange."

SECTION SEVEN

EXPLORING CLASSES AND MEMORIES

EXPLORING

"Jonathan, I have read my entire one half of the Dr. Phenom files, and they are so fascinating. Did you know he teaches or has colleagues put on classes on all kinds of *supernatural* stuff?"

"Yes. I am becoming aware of that. You will also be fascinated by the stories in the collection I am reading, Ana."

"I am ready. Let's exchange so we are both on the same page, so to speak."

"I have all day Thursday. Let's plan on discussing our findings then, Ana."

THURSDAY

"Wow. This Dr. Phenom is into everything, isn't he, Jonathan."

"Well, he has a reputation of being a *know it all*."

"I understand some people don't like his condescending attitude."

"He *has* published numerous books on all of these subjects, Ana."

"But, Jonathan, *why* is he so insistent on meeting you; and *why* are you avoiding him?"

"To answer *that*, I will simply say I am loyal to Dr. Mesmer."

"I don't understand."

"Dr. Mesmer knows Dr. Phenom and advised me *not* to connect with him at this time in our sessions."

"Well, that seems a little odd, doesn't it, Jonathan?"

"Yes, but I will honor Dr. Mesmer's wishes."

"You're very honorable, Jonathan."

"Yes, but I have a request of you, Ana."

"And what might that be?"

"I want you to sign up for some of those classes that he heads up."

"Sure. That's exciting. Wow. Here we go again. I was about to suggest we sign up for classes."

"You. Just you, Ana. I need to analyze this all *impartially*."

"I am all on board, Jonathan."

SIGNED UP

"Wow. I am kind of excited, Jonathan. I signed up for three different classes."

"They're all exciting prospects, aren't they. So which ones did you sign up for, Ana?"

"The first is *Lucid Dreaming* on Mondays, then *Regression Therapy* on Wednesdays, and *Tarot Cards* on Fridays."

"I take it that the Gypsy lady at the fairgrounds influenced that last choice."

"I may take up *Meditation* after I finish these courses."

"You're certainly jumping right in there, Ana."

"I'm kind of thrilled by all of this, Jonathan."

"Yes. This will also be therapeutic for *me*."

"Yes, Jonathan, life is becoming exciting, isn't it"

"Just a *little* more exciting. It has *always* been pretty awesome since I met you, Ana."

"Oh, … thank you, Jonathan."

NEED SUPPLIES

"Jonathan, I need supplies."

"You're getting started, I believe."

"I sure am ... and I am *excited*."

"I'm listening, Ana."

"It was good ... no ... it was *great*! They had a long term *lucid dreamer* tell us some fantastic dream stories about his escapades. ... I need to get a *dream diary* and a *'Can You Believe It'* ...an eye mask that can tell when you're in *REM* sleep."

"*REM* sleep. ... That stands for Rapid Eye Movement when you're dreaming."

"Yes, Jonathan. The eye mask alerts you to realize you're dreaming and wake up to the fact that you're in a dream."

"You're having fun with this, aren't you Ana."

"Jonathan, I will teach you all that I learn so you can appease your special patient Angela."

"Ana, that sounds like a wonderful plan to me. I look forward to your tutoring."

"And, Jonathan, Kathie went with me. They let her right into the class after they had her sign up."

"So, how was it? What did she think?"

"We have to purchase and read Dr. Phenom's book."

"Your impression was …?"

"The instructor started a little slow in explaining it. Some people will get good at *lucid dreaming*, and some people won't get it at all. … But, like I said, I have to start a *dream journal*; and that sounds like work, Jonathan."

"What did Kathie think of it?"

"Oh … she is really into it. She already uses her *dream journal*. I ordered a *dream eye mask*. I think that will be more exciting."

"When do you do the *regression* class, Ana?"

"That's the one you are most interested in. I will do that beginning Wednesday, Jonathan."

"Yes. I will be anxious to see what *that* is all about."

JONATHAN'S GOING AWAY

"Kathie, … Jonathan's going away."

"Jonathan going away? Did you guys have a disagreement, Ana?"

"No. Nothing like that. We never fight."

"What then? What are you talking about?"

"He has informed me that he will be gone for 3 or 4 weeks, Kathie."

"Ok. What's going on?"

"He has been challenged."

"This is crazy talk, Ana. Get to the point. What does *being challenged* mean?"

"He is having a very difficult time dealing with what has transpired with the lady."

"You mean that psychic lady Angela? … Excuse me … I mean that … *so called* … psychic lady."

"You're still very skeptical, aren't you, Kathie."

"Yes. Yes. Very much … as you also should be, Ana."

"Well, please don't relay your feelings to Jonathan. He is conflicted enough."

"Yes, I sense that he is very conflicted; so I will keep my thoughts to myself."

"*That* is very important, Kathie, or I won't be able to share with you concerning him."

"I understand. I completely understand, Ana. So what is this about Jonathan going away?"

"He is going on some sort of retreat."

"What kind of retreat?"

"A very far away retreat."

"And where might that be, Ana?"

"The Himalayas. Tibet … to some monastery I guess."

"Wow. This is getting mysterious."

"That is a good way of putting it, Kathie. ... *Life* is getting mysterious."

WHAT WAS IT LIKE?

(The girls discuss another class session ...)

"Kathie, what was it like?"

"Ana, do you remember when he asked me to recall or remember my 10th birthday at 12 noon?"

"Yes. I was sitting in the front row ... right in front of where you and the instructor were talking."

"I remember looking right at you, Ana, trying to recall what we were doing back then."

"Yes. Yes. I couldn't remember either; but I know we have shared every birthday since I first met you, Kathie."

"I was looking for ... *you* ... to remember."

"I just shook my head. ... No help from me."

"But then he did what I think was *hypnosis*."

"Yes. Yes, Kathie. And you started telling all about that day; and, as you did, … I remembered right along with you."

"That was very impressive, don't you think?"

"Yes, it was *very* impressive; and I have to take notes on all of this as Jonathan instructed me to do."

"You better take detailed notes. You know Jonathan is very thorough."

"Yes, you better help me with those details, Kathie."

"I will. I will."

HAPPY TO BE HOME

(three weeks later, Jonathan is home …)

"Jonathan, I am so happy that you're home."

"I am happy to be home, Ana."

"Did you miss me a little?"

"I didn't have time to miss *anything*."

"What are the Himalayas like, Jonathan?"

"Beautiful … but cold!"

"Well, did you achieve what you went for?"

"Very much so. It was fruitful."

"Do you mind us talking about your adventure?"

"I'm sorry, Ana, … but I can't. ….. Some things I can't share with anyone, even you."

"I understand, Jonathan. Just know I am here for you with anything you may need me for."

"I will need some time to gather my thoughts, Ana."

"I understand. I completely understand."

ANASTACIA'S DIARY

Dear Diary .....

Understand? ..... Whatever does that mean? ..... I totally don't understand. ..... I have no idea what is happening to my man, ... how to be there for him. ..... Distant. ..... That is what his demeanor is ..... distant.

NOTES

"Jonathan, you asked me to take notes."

"How did that go, Ana?"

"I think I captured everything that I thought would be important for you to know."

"I am looking forward to our discussion, as soon as I feel ready."

"How are you feeling, Jonathan? You seem distant to me."

"The trip was very exhausting. I endured some experiences I can't talk about. Give me a little time, and I am sure I will recuperate, Ana."

"Whenever you feel it's appropriate, Jonathan."

COUNSEL

"Kathie, I need your counsel."

"I know it's about Jonathan, isn't it Ana."

"He is talking in his sleep."

"Did he ever do that before?"

"Never. He always slept so peacefully, Kathie."

"What are you concerned about?"

"I have been jotting down his mumblings."

"You listen to his dreaming, I take it?"

"Yes. It keeps me awake, … and what is coming out is intriguing."

"I'm listening, Ana. Go on. Like what?"

"I believe he is *lucid dreaming*."

"Do you think he learned how to do that in Tibet?"

"I believe he did … and I believe he also did some very advanced stuff."

"How did you come to that conclusion, Ana?"

"I ordered advanced information about Tibet monasteries, Kathie."

"You mean from your *special agency* that can get anything for a price?"

"That's what I did … and Jonathan can never know."

"I totally understand, Ana."

CAN I SHARE SOMETHING?

(The girls continue to discuss Jonathan's behavior …)

"Kathie, can I share something with you?"

"What do you want to share, Ana?"

"Jonathan."

"You want to share Jonathan?"

"No. No. No. It's not like that. I want to share what he is doing now."

"And what might that be?"

"I think he is communicating."

"Ana, can you make some sense here."

"Just listen. Jonathan is talking in his sleep, and I think he is *lucid*."

"So you think he is … *lucid dreaming*?"

"Yes. Yes. And I want to know if it's ethical to listen in, Kathie."

"That's a good question, isn't it, Ana."

"He is very verbal, and you can almost grasp the content of what is being talked about."

"So … you have overheard what he is saying?"

"Yes. Yes. And it is all very intriguing, and I have been taking notes."

"Can I see your notes, Ana."

"I have to ponder this, Kathie. Even though you're my best friend, I am not sure if I can share personal stuff."

"Is it *that personal*?"

"Yes … and *more* than that."

"Ana, you decide if you want me in on this."

"Kathie, thanks for understanding."

ANA IS CHOSEN

"Jonathan, I have been informed that Dr. Phenom will be present at my next hypnosis regression class. What do you want me to do?"

"That could be interesting. Will he be observing or participating, Ana?"

"I was told he would be the instructor, and everyone in the class is excited to have him teach."

"Well, this could be our chance to see how good he is. Are you willing to be a volunteer for his regression session?"

"That will be exciting. I will sit right up front. Everyone seemed to be reluctant, so I will be enthusiastic. I'm sure he will choose me, Jonathan."

(later that day at class…)

"Kathie, Jonathan wants me to be chosen for participation in the regression session. Do you want to sit up front with me?"

"Look, Ana, they're preparing a chair for a participant. Why don't you just go up and sit in that chair."

"Do you think I should? ... Yes. I am going to do it."

"Ana, I'll just sit back here. There are already a lot of people here."

"Wish me luck, Kathie."

"Go do it, Ana."

(up front ...)

"Hi. My name is Ana. I would like to volunteer."

"My. My. You are an attractive lady, if I may say so. Just sit yourself down. I think Dr. Phenom will very much approve of you."

*(Dr. Phenom enters
and addresses the class ...)*

"May I introduce myself ... I am Dr. Phenom. I am very privileged to be your instructor this evening, and I see we already have a volunteer. And how might we address you, Young Lady?"

"My name is Anastacia Romanov."

"And, Anastacia, is it correct that we have not met before?"

"Yes, Dr. Phenom, this is our first time meeting."

"Anastacia, have you ever experienced *hypnosis*?"

"No. I have heard about this sort of thing, but my first experience was last week at this class with your colleague. I was impressed."

"Well, class, I am going to give Anastacia some hypnotic instruction; and if all of my audience will remain as quiet as possible. Thank you."

(Doctor administers hypnotic induction …)

"And now, Anastacia, I want you to delve deep into the recesses of your memory bank. I want you to access a very important event in this life or an important event from a previous life. … This will happen … now."

"No! No! Please NO!! … Run Tatiana! … RUN!!"

"Anastacia, you will come up NOW! … Fully awake … all memories gone. When I clap my hands twice, all memories of this session will be gone." … (*clap! … clap!*)

"Well, audience and Anastacia, sometimes we must address traumatic memories such as Anastacia's in a private session. I'm sure you all understand. I will now let my colleague take over this class."

(a little later after the class is over ...)

"Are you ok, Ana? What do you make of what happened?"

"I don't know, Kathie. I don't remember anything, but Dr. Phenom wants me to schedule a private session with him."

"That session was dramatic. You scared everybody when you screamed, Ana."

"I don't remember anything, Kathie."

(Jonathan joins the conversation ...)

"Jonathan, I don't know what to tell you."

"What do you mean by that, Ana? Did you participate?"

"I think I did."

"You *think you did*. ... What does that mean?"

"Let Kathie tell you. I'm a little confused."

"Ok, Kathie, what happened in class?"

"Jonathan, I don't know how to explain it. Ana did as you asked and volunteered."

"So what happened? What transpired during the hypnosis demonstration?"

"Nothing. No ... that's not true. It didn't *get* that far."

"Kathie, you're not explaining it very well."

"Ana screamed and screamed really loud. It startled everyone. Even Dr. Phenom jumped."

"Then what?"

"Then he quickly did something to bring her out of it, instructing her to remember *nothing*."

"Ana, is that what happened?"

"I don't know. I ... *don't* ... remember anything, Jonathan."

"Remember, Ana, ... you scheduled a private session with Dr. Phenom next Friday at 1:00."

"Thank you, Kathie. Yes, I guess we will find out answers on Friday."

"More pieces to the puzzle."

(after Ana's Friday session with Dr.Phenom...)

"Ana, I have done research, and it is remarkable what I have found out."

"You researched about what I was remembering?"

"Yes. Was it as terrifying as you described it was?"

"How would *you* like to remember your whole family being killed ... murdered! ... It was terrifying."

"Well, you also told names ... places ... people ... Do you remember that?"

"Yes. I certainly do. It was all very clear."

"Who was *Tatiana*, the name you screamed out? And do you remember your father's name?"

"Tatiana was my favorite sister, and we were very close. ... My father's name was *Nicholas*, and he was very important. We lived in Russia."

"Yes, I would say the *Emperor ... Czar ... of Russia ...* was kind of important, Ana."

ANASTACIA'S DIARY

Dear Diary .....

Where is this path taking me? ... Did I choose?, ... or ... does ... or ... is ... my destiny being chosen for me? ..... Am I being led to who knows where ... or ... to who knows what?? ..... As they say, ... so far so good. ..... Jonathan, ... hold my hand. ... Never let go ... my perfect man.

PLEASE PLEASE

"Ana, why is Jonathan grilling you so hard about your memories in Russia?"

"Because he is investigating whether the memories I am having can be collaborated with documented recorded history."

"But why is he so obsessed?"

"Because he has been going through hypnotic regression sessions with Dr. Mesmer; and when he is finally informed about the results of his sessions, he will *already* have concluded one way or the other about the possible truth and validity of what is discovered."

"That is a whole lot of *mumbo jumbo* there, Girl."

"You have to take this seriously, Kathie. We have to take this seriously if we're going to be there for Jonathan."

"I guess you're right, … but this is getting pretty deep here."

"I know, Kathie, … but this is pretty important to Jonathan."

"I guess I understand, Ana, … and I will keep my thoughts to myself."

"Please. Please. For both me *and* Jonathan."

MORE MEMORIES

"Ana, you look engrossed. What are you writing about?"

"Like I told you before, Jonathan wants me to write out all of the memories I keep on having on his notepads."

"He is going to need a whole new set of notepads the way you have been writing there."

"Yes, I know. I keep remembering more and more. It's almost like reliving another life, Kathie."

"Well, Ana, ... that is exactly what you're doing, isn't it."

"Yes, I guess so. Some of what I am remembering was very terrifying."

"Well, like you told me before, Ana, it was a good thing Dr. Phenom gave you that hypnotic command that you would remember things in a *calm passive state of recall.*"

"Yes. Yes. I could not handle all of what I'm remembering if it was presented any other way."

"Is your memory conjuring up anything interesting?"

"Are you kidding me? All kinds of stuff, Kathie."

"Ok Girl. Let's hear something interesting."

"First, … I was *not* wanted. … I was a disappointment."

"*Not wanted*, Ana?"

"I was a girl. They needed a boy to keep the monarchy going."

"That had to be hard to take."

"No. No. I was treated very well, but I was aware that I should have been a boy. That's all."

"Interesting memories. Keep talking, Ana."

"I keep remembering more details, … more about wars and strange people."

"That sounds interesting. What is this about *strange* people?"

"Well, my little brother was sick … very sick. And he was to be groomed to someday inherit the monarchy, Kathie."

"What was strange about that?"

"They brought in a very big strange man named Grigori Rasputin. I think he was a monk or mystic faith healer or something like that, but he seemed to be able to help my little brother. I remember I did not like him; he liked his liquor too much."

"Wow, Ana. You really *are* getting into this recalling of memories, aren't you."

"Yes. They are flooding in, … and I have to take notes for Jonathan."

"Well, you seem to be taking care of that all right."

"I hope Jonathan approves, Kathie."

"He will. He will, Ana."

PRINCESS?

"Ana. Ana. This is so interesting. Do you know what your *regression session* revealed?"

"When Dr. Phenom repeated my private hypnotic regression session with me being a *passive observer* this time, it was *still* very traumatic and very real to me, Kathie."

"Ana, what you are experiencing in those sessions are a part of documented Russian history."

"Yes, ... that seems to be so. As long as I can remain only a *passive* observer of my regression memories, I would like to explore this further."

"What does Jonathan think of all this, Ana?"

"Jonathan is very enthusiastic about the regression sessions. They seem to validate his experiences with Dr. Mesmer. ... And, Dr. Phenom is recording our sessions; and I will be receiving a copy of every session, Kathie."

"That will be great. We can compare your recorded past life memories to the historical documented facts, Ana."

"Yes. I am sure Jonathan will investigate everything … to verify *if* it's factual."

"What do you think Jonathan thinks? Will he want to engage with Dr. Phenom?"

"I am sure Jonathan is on top of this. We will just wait and see, won't we, Kathie."

"Yes, Ana. Just wait and see, *Princess*."

"*Princess*??"

"Yes, Ana, … if your past life father was a king or czar, you *were* a princess."

"Kathie, you need to put emphasis on …*WERE*."

VALIDATION

"Well, Jonathan, what is your conclusion here?"

"Ana, I have been very thorough in my investigation. There is a lot of recorded history on *Nicholas Alexandrovich Romanov*. He was born May 6, 1868 and lived until his family was murdered on July 17, 1918. He had five children … four girls: Olga, Tatiana, Maria, and coincidentally, *Anastasia*."

"He had a daughter named *Anastasia*? What do you make of that?"

"That *is* something, isn't it. This could be the validation I am looking for, Ana."

"I hope so, Jonathan. I hope so."

SECTION EIGHT

A SISTER

A SISTER

"Ana, what was all that about last night? You screamed so loud you woke me up."

"I am so sorry, Kathie. I think I am getting the *lucid dreaming* and *regression* memories mixed up."

"I thought Dr. Phenom gave you *post hypnotic instructions* to recall your past life memories in a calm passive way."

"Well, last night I dreamed I was with my sister Tatiana; and we were running away from the Bolsheviks, and I fell and told her not to stop. *Keep running!*"

"That has to be a tough dream to recall, Ana."

"It wasn't a *dream*, … it was a *memory*. Tatiana and I were close, and I have something that I don't know how to explain."

"Do you want to go to those *dark* memories with me, Ana?"

"Yes, Kathie. I have to talk with someone, and I think Jonathan has too much of his own to deal with right now."

"You know, Ana, I am always here for you."

"But, Kathie, you have a different set of beliefs; and what I am experiencing is *very* real to me."

"Yes, you're right. I *am* having a hard time believing all of this is *real* or *factual* or just *imagination gone wild*."

"See, Kathie. See. I don't believe you can be unbiased."

"But, Ana, don't you *need* someone to be grounded? To make sure this isn't just *imagination gone wild*?"

"I love you, Kathie, … but you may not be what I need right now."

"I don't agree. I am *exactly* what you need, Ana."

"I have to think about this. Please be patient. We will talk later."

ANASTACIA'S DIARY

Dear Diary .....

Who do I talk to? ... Crazy thoughts. ... Am I dreaming? ... Lucid dreaming. ... My memories. ... So real. ... So very very real. ... Are they real? ... Or as Kathie says ... imagination gone wild? ... A good way of explaining ... just ... wild.

ANOTHER SESSION

"Dr. Phenom, this is Anastacia Romanov. I would like to schedule another consultation session with you."

"How about this Friday at 2:00? ... I will set aside two hours."

"I will be there, Dr. Phenom."

(Friday at 2:00 ...)

"I see that you are very punctual, Ms. Romanov."

"Please, Doctor, would you mind addressing me as *Ana*?"

"I can accommodate you with that request, Ana."

"Dr. Phenom, I am having a hard time dealing with what has transpired in our sessions so far."

"That, Young Lady, is a very normal reaction to anything that is *out of your comfort zone*, so to speak."

"Let me get right to the point, Doctor, ... are these memories that I am experiencing *real*?"

"Well, Ana, the question begs an answer from *you*. ... What do *you* think?"

"I think you're not answering my question."

"I am not trying to be contrite here; but only *you* can truthfully answer that question, Ana."

"So how do I get to the truth of the matter, Doctor?"

"My answer is simple. ... We schedule more regression sessions. We delve deeper until you're satisfied."

"Ok, Dr. Phenom. I am willing. Let's do it."

"We will schedule six more sessions. Will that be satisfactory with you?"

"Yes. Thank you Dr. Phenom."

AT ANOTHER SESSION

"I am a little early, Dr. Phenom. I see you're still with your patient."

"Yes. I am just finishing up. It will be just a few minutes."

(a few minutes later ...)

"Dr. Phenom, I get so excited about our sessions. I always arrive a little too early."

"That, Young Lady, is a compliment to our endeavor here. I very much look forward to our regression sessions. They have become very special to me, Ana."

"Don't you have other interesting patients?"

"*All* my patients are interesting; but you seem to be accessing, with your memories, information that can be verified ... and *that* is of great importance to me."

"Yes, I am baffled by my memories having historical value."

"Well, this is what seems to transpire here; and I must ask for your permission to publish our findings. This could be the validation this kind of research needs."

"If this is beneficial to you, Dr. Phenom, I fully approve."

"You no doubt will someday have to autograph my new book dedicated to our research, Ana."

UPGRADE

"Dr. Phenom, you wanted to see me?"

"Is it still appropriate to address you as *Ana*?"

"Of course, Doctor, but I still prefer to address *you* as *Dr. Phenom*."

"I will accept that, Ana; but at this time I believe it to be important to have an open, honest, and deep conversation. Are you willing to participate in that with me?"

"I really don't know where you are going with this, Dr. Phenom."

"First, Ana, are you in agreement to *upgrade* your status?"

"Again, I don't understand."

"You have obtained files on me, Ana. Have you read them all?"

"Dr. Phenom, I don't know how to answer that."

"Ana, like I said … open, honest, and deep conversation."

"Could you possibly explain to me *what* you know, Doctor."

"I know *everything*; and for you to be open and honest, … *you* … need to know that I know."

"Doctor, would you be willing to prove that to me?"

"First, Ana, with your permission, I would like to upgrade your status in the *society*."

"What does *that* mean?"

"That means you will hold a higher status, Ana."

"Doctor, there are complications. Can I think about this?"

"You want to confer with Kathie … *and* Jonathan? You will have two days."

AT HOME

"Kathie, … Dr. Phenom knows."

"Ana, … I am taking a nap. … Can't this wait?"

"No. No. ... I don't know if I should talk to you ... or Jonathan ..."

"Ana, you know Jonathan is out of town at that very secluded meditation retreat."

"That's why I have to talk to somebody, Kathie."

"Am I just ... *somebody*?"

"Please, Kathie. This is serious. I really don't know what I should do."

"Do you *really* want to talk to me?"

"No. You may not be the one I should talk to first, Kathie."

"Do you want to wait for Jonathan?"

"No. No. I only have two days, ... but you have signed in as a member of my special agency. Right? Right, Kathie??"

"Yes, you're right. But what does *that* mean, Ana?"

"It means I can talk to you. Yes. Yes. I can talk to *you*."

"Talk then."

THE FILES

"Ana, your assignment was to read all the files you have on me."

"Dr. Phenom, I received a lot of files on you."

"I know that, Ana. I had to approve all those files you have received."

"You had to *what*??"

"Yes. I am going to attempt to gain your trust by revealing my status in the *society*."

"I take it that you hold a position like head of the FBI or CIA. Am I reading into this correctly, Dr. Phenom?"

"Young Lady, you are reading into this … *very* … correctly."

"What are you suggesting here, Dr. Phenom?"

"I am suggesting that you *really* understand what possibly could be transpiring here, Ana."

"Well you certainly have a way of expressing things."

"You, Young Lady, may be instrumental in mankind's destiny."

"What in heaven's name are you referring to?"

"Ana, I need to know if you're religious."

"That question catches me off guard, Doctor. I really don't know how to answer that."

"Ok. I realize I am moving too fast. Let's approach this by upgrading your standing in the *society*."

"Again, Dr. Phenom, I really need to converse with Jonathan Masters, my boyfriend."

"I very much know who he is … or *thinks* he knows who he … *really is*."

"That talk is very disturbing to me, Dr. Phenom."

"I understand, Ms. Anastacia Romanov."

CONFUSED

"Kathie. Kathie. Kathie!"

"You are disturbed, aren't you Ana."

"Boy, you can say that again. I really don't know how to begin."

"You came right home and went to bed, and now you awaken still upset. Let's hear your story."

"He is a very powerful, condescending, strong-willed man."

"Now who could you be referring to, Ana?"

"This is serious, Kathie. He said something that disturbed me."

"So … an explanation would be helpful here."

"He wanted me to be *upgraded*."

"*Upgraded*? Explain, Ana."

"That *secret society* thing. It is really scary to me. You have to very much abide by all of their rules."

"So … I take it you did not accept, Ana?"

"I told him I had to ponder this; and he said it was a big step, and he seemed to understand."

"Seemed to understand?"

"Yes. I really don't know what he is thinking. You really can't read him, Kathie. I think all that information we received on him was what he *wanted* us to believe."

"So … you think he is the head of … *all this*?"

"That is exactly what I think … and there is more."

"I'm listening, Ana."

"He said something about Jonathan."

"What did he say about Jonathan?"

"I can't tell you right now."

"Why not?"

"I have my reasons, … and I believe the way *you* believe. … It would only confuse things more, Kathie."

"Ana, I don't think you could make me any *more* confused."

BLIND LOVE

"Are you still contemplating?"

"Very much so, Kathie. I have to figure this all out, and I only have *one* more day to decide."

"Have you considered every possible outcome, Ana?"

"The way I see it, I *should* accept a higher position in *the society*. Then I can have access to what Jonathan desires."

"*But*, Ana, … at what cost to *you*?"

"That is the chance I will have to take for the man I love."

"I am not sure whether that is noble … or foolish. But, as they say, *love is blind*."

DECISION

"Dr. Phenom, I have made a decision."

"And your decision *is* … ?"

"I will *accept* a higher position in *the society*."

"Ana, you will be contacted by initiates with the credentials to facilitate that endeavor. We will have no further contact until this mission is completed. *Is that understood?*"

"That is understood, Dr. Phenom."

I APPROVE

"Kathie, I wish Jonathan was here to consult on this."

"You really had little choice; and I approve of your decision, Ana."

"I think I made the right decision under the conditions I had to deal with, don't you agree, Kathie?"

"I totally agree, but you have to be very diligent in how you handle things from here on out."

"I am going to rely on your advice, Kathie, I trust you."

"Ana, I am with you all the way … as I am sure Jonathan will be."

"What do you think will happen next, Kathie?"

"Ana, I guess we wait until you're contacted."

(days later …)

"Ana, you have a letter here that needs your signature to be accepted."

"I will be right there, Kathie."

"So this must be it, … what we've been waiting for."

"Look it says *PRIVATE – TO BE OPENED BY ANASTACIA ROMANOV.*"

"Well, let's just open this and see what we have here."

"Look at this. Is *this* supposed to scare somebody?"

"Well, it's kind of scary to *me*."

"Disregard that skull figure and open it up, Kathie."

"A black envelope with black paper and white printed instructions … Is this supposed to be intimidating?"

"Well, Kathie, if it *is* … it's working for me."

"Look. It's instructions for what you are to do, Ana."

"What are the instructions? What do they say?"

"You are to go at exactly 12 noon to this address, … you are to be dressed in all black, … no perfume, … no lipstick, … no fingernail polish, … no jewelry, … no purse."

"Look, Kathie, there are further instructions … It says to ring the bell three times … hesitate … then ring the bell three more times. And all *that* concludes the instructions for me."

"You're not going to do this, Ana. This is *crazy* stuff."

"Kathie, this is my decision. I have already made my decision, and I will follow through with my decision."

"I really don't know what to say."

"Kathie, please don't say anything."

BACK HOME

"Ana. Ana. I have been so worried. … Are you ok? Are you all right? Oh … oh … I am so glad you're back home."

"Kathie, just let me get out of this black dress. I will never wear black again."

"Ana, why are you so calm?"

"Why shouldn't I be calm, Kathie?"

"Why shouldn't I just bop you. You better start talking … and *fast!*"

"Look at you, Kathie, … all upset; and you're supposed to be the rational one here."

"Come on, Ana, … no time for joking."

"Relax, Kathie. Just relax. Everything went extremely well."

"Come on, Ana. I'm serious. I was panicking all afternoon. I need details."

"Ok. So I was a little scared too, … maybe a *lot* scared; … but it turned out to be unwarranted fear."

"Come on. *Details!* Come on, Ana."

"When I arrived at the address in the letter, a couple of men asked me to get into a waiting limousine and put on a mask over my eyes. I was taken somewhere else in the car. When we finally arrived, I was instructed to take off the mask; and I was escorted in through a door. It was pitch dark, but I could see way in front of me a candle burning ... lots of them; and they had a sweet waxy perfume smell."

"Was this some kind of ritual, Ana?"

"Yes, it was, ... but it was *not* spooky at all. ... *But* it was definitely a ritual."

"Were you scared?"

"*Yes* and *no*, Kathie."

"What kind of answer is *that*?"

"Yes, I was very scared at first; ... but they told me to drink this very sweet drink, and I did. After that, *no*, I was actually very pleasantly happy."

"They *drugged* you, in other words."

"No, I wouldn't put it exactly like that; I very much liked what happened, Kathie."

"So ... what happened then?"

"I'm sorry. ... I can't tell you."

"You're still a little high, aren't you, Ana?"

"I have to take a nap now. I will talk with you later."

"Yes, Ana. You need to sleep this off. Good night, Ana."

CONSULT WITH YOUR DAD

"Kathie, if I tell you something, will you promise not to scoff or laugh or anything?"

"No. No. I can't promise anything. The way things are happening, I don't know *how* to react, Ana."

"I know this is confusing to you. It's very confusing to me also."

"You know we are dealing with some very crazy goings on here, Ana."

"I agree. ... I think I need advice counseling, Kathie."

"Why don't you consult your dad?"

"*He* is not my *dad*. He is just my *father*, ... my *biological father*, whose wife doesn't want me in their life at all, Kathie."

"Ana, you keep saying that; and I don't believe that at all. I know that Dr. Mesmer, your *biological* father, has been trying to reach out to you; and you don't respond to his calls."

"That's because I don't want to interfere with their happy marriage."

"Did you forget that his wife left him, Ana?"

"Yes, I know that, … and all because of me."

"Come on, Ana. You know better than that. Doesn't *he* have a say in this?"

"What are you suggesting I do, Kathie?"

"It wouldn't hurt you to just talk with him."

"Kathie, I wouldn't know how to act with him after my outburst."

"He would probably understand. Don't forget, he is also a very good psychiatrist."

"I am so conflicted. I don't know what I should do."

"Why don't I do it for you, Ana."

"Do what?"

"Well, I'll contact Dr. Mesmer and make some excuse like I need counseling; and somehow I'll determine how he perceives all of this."

"Do you think that's the way to handle this, Kathie?"

"The more I think about it, yes. Yes I do, Ana. Just let me handle this, ok?"

"Ok Kathie."

THE COUNSEL

"It's been awhile. How have you been doing, Kathie?"

"Well, Dr. Mesmer, as you very well know, I am best friends with your daughter."

"It's going to take some time to get used to *that* statement, Kathie."

"Well, Dr. Mesmer, get used to it. I mean business here."

"Ha. Ha. I see you want to reverse roles here. Let's see what you have to say, Young Lady."

"Well, Doctor, as I see it this situation is not being dealt with properly."

"I am listening, Young Lady, … very intently listening."

"Well, I guess I am through with *my* lecturing. Now I should probably listen to what *you* have to say, Doctor."

"That was amusing, and it certainly took the edge off… *is it my turn now*?"

"Yes, Dr. Mesmer. It's your turn."

"Ok. Let's analyze the situation here."

"I am listening, Dr. Mesmer."

"We have *two* concerns here … the Jonathan *regression* issue … and the *biological father and daughter* issue. Am I correct on that so far?"

"Yes, Doctor, you are very correct on that."

"So, which do we deal with first, Kathie?"

"First, I am just here to *break the ice* so to speak."

"You're talking about Ms. Romanov?"

"I am talking about your daughter, Doctor. Your DAUGHTER!"

"Yes. Yes. Calm down. I just wanted to see your reaction, Kathie."

"Well, you certainly got it, didn't you."

"I think the person I need in this chair is Ana."

"*That* is what I needed to hear, Dr. Mesmer. I will make *that* happen."

"Thank you, Kathie."

THE MEETING

"Good morning, Dr. Mesmer."

"Good morning, Ana."

(silence ...)

"Is it ok if I call you *Dr. Mesmer*?"

"Most people do."

"You know what I mean."

"Yes, I guess this is supposed to be a little awkward, isn't it."

"Does it have to be?"

"What do *you* think, Ana?"

"Doctor, can I ask for something?"

"What might that be?"

"I could use a hug. Would that be too inappropriate?"

"Well, why don't we just find out."

(hug time ...)

"I feel a little better."

"So do I, Ana. ….. Well, let's get right down to business. … So I understand you undertook the *initiation*."

"How do you know about that, Dr. Mesmer?"

"I hold a position that had to approve of *that* action, Ana."

"So this *secret society* is not so secret after all."

"You're wrong about that. Only top ranked members are privileged to important affairs, Ana."

"I could not see all that transpired; it was so very dark. Were you there, Doctor?"

"I was *and* so were many other prominent members. It was a bigger affair than you realize."

"Why did they place me on that big fancy chair?"

"That, Ana, has significance. That chair, as you call it, is actually a *throne*, ... and few have the privilege of sitting there."

"Why is this happening to *me*?"

"You are being groomed for something special, Ana."

"I don't know how to take all of this, Doctor."

"My advice to you, Ana, is to just, as they say, *go with the flow*."

"That seems to be too simple."

"You just have to trust me here. Ana, it is all working as it should."

"Ok, Doctor. *Father*. I will trust you."

(Later that day, Kathie and Ana talk ...)

"So, Ana, ... let's hear it. How did it go with Dr. Mesmer?"

"You truly are my best friend, Kathie; and you *do* give the best advice *ever*."

"I take that as in *it went very well*."

"Yes. At first, as expected, it was awkward; … but then I suggested a *hug*."

"That was a great gesture on your part. Very well done, Ana."

"And there is more …"

"I'm listening."

"I addressed him as *Father*."

"Wow. That is perfect. More than I could have asked for. I'm proud of you, Ana."

"Yes. Yes. I am pretty satisfied too. Thank you, Kathie, for being the best friend ever."

"Best friends *forever*."

DREAMING

"Kathie, this *lucid dreaming* is becoming crazy."

"Ana, what are you dreaming about to say something like that?"

"You know in my *past life regression* I remembered being very close to one of my sisters in that life time …"

"As I recall you had three sisters and a brother, … right, Ana?"

"Yes. And I was especially close to Tatiana. We did everything together, Kathie."

"I remember your terrifying story."

"I have been dreaming or recalling memories I had with her. We were very close. You might even say *bonded together*."

"That is very very interesting, isn't it?"

"It's more than interesting, Kathie. I believe she followed me or came with me over here to this present time."

"Wow. What are you saying, Ana?"

"She is here. Jonathan saw her."

"This is some crazy stuff you're *imagining* or *dreaming*, Ana."

"No, Kathie, this is *real*. I feel it. I know it. I think Tatiana is my twin sister over here."

"Wow. Wow. All I can say is this is getting crazier by the day."

"I know. I know. It's hard to believe, but I somehow know now that Jonathan saw *Tatiana* in New York when he thought it was me."

"Wow, Ana, … this really *is* getting far out there."

"You may not be the one I need to talk to, Kathie. I love you, but you're *way* too skeptical."

"Oh don't cry, Ana. I'm sorry. I really am. I'll try to *not* be skeptical."

"Kathie, I want my sister back. I want Tatiana back."

"You still have *me*."

"I want *both* of you."

SHE SCREAMS AGAIN

"Ana, are you sure you're ok with all this?"

"So you heard me, Kathie?"

"I'm sure the *whole* complex heard you, Ana. It was a terrifying scream."

"Oh. I hope not. That is embarrassing."

"You took your notepad and tape recorder to bed with you, I assume."

"Yes. I have it all on tape."

"*That* should be listened to with *earmuffs* on."

"Was it *that* loud really, Kathie?"

"I am serious, Ana. I thought someone was killing you."

"They *were*. They *really were*. It was so real."

"So… were you *lucid dreaming*?"

"I don't know. I think it was part *past memory recall* and a very *very* real *lucid dream*."

"That has to be hard to deal with, ... horrible memories like that, Ana."

"Yes, I am going to have to be reinforced with the ... *passive recall instruction*."

"Again, this must be hard on you."

"It is both kind of *scary* and *exhilarating* at the same time. I believe I am recalling *real* memories, Kathie."

"I don't know if I want to listen to your recording or not. It was frightening."

"Do you think I should erase last night's recording session?"

"No. No. This is very valuable. Jonathan will want to hear it."

"So do I. ... When I *wake up*, ... I can't recall what transpired in my dreams."

"I bet that is because Dr. Phenom told you to erase your *recall*. *Remember?* At your first session with him."

"Yes. Now that you mention it, that *was* his instruction. I will have to rely on the tape recordings."

"You better safeguard those recordings, Ana."

"I will Kathie. I will."

HE DOESN'T TELL ME ANYTHING

(the girls are talking after Ana's recent session with Dr. Phenom ...)

"He doesn't tell me anything. I have to figure this out on my own, Kathie."

"You don't have to figure *anything* out on your own, Ana. You have *me*."

"Oh, I know I do; but you are always so skeptical."

"I am just trying to be *rational*. You need to be a little skeptical yourself, Ana."

"That is exactly the point I am trying to make here. *You* are not experiencing what I am experiencing, ... what *I* am going through."

"What is it you want me to do, Ana? What more can I do?"

"Kathie, why are you so reluctant to do the *hypnotic regression session*, as I am doing?"

"Because *someone* has to be totally awake and alert and, ... as you say, ... be *skeptical* of all this."

"But, Kathie, you can't *know* until you experience it for yourself."

"Yes, ... but it's possible that you are being *programmed* into false beliefs, Ana; and that is why I need to be *biased* here."

"I am not going to be able to get through to you, am I?"

"You already have, and I am totally here for you, Ana."

"I need my *old* sister back. I could talk to Tatiana about *anything*."

"Tatiana is a *dream* sister, ... or just a memory, Ana."

"See ... she is real, *very* real to me. I keep having more memories. ... I keep reliving over and over those last moments."

"Ana, that cannot be good that you are in that loop with those tragic memories of Tatiana."

"I believe that she is *here*, … and I need to find her, Kathie."

"So, you are of the mindset that Jonathan saw *her* in New York when he thought it was *you*?"

"That is the rational explanation of my deep feeling that … she is here, … over *here* in this lifetime."

"Well, I certainly don't know how to explain all that; and to tell the truth, I am a little jealous."

"Kathie, try to understand what I *don't* understand."

"There you go again, … making sense out of something that *doesn't* make sense."

"Kathie, don't be jealous. *Please* don't be jealous."

"Ana, I am just being honest with you. I am very *very* jealous."

"I need you, Kathie. I *really* need you at this time."

"Ana, you have me. You will *always* have me."

ANA'S GYPSY READING

*(Ana visits Gypsies again to try
to get some answers ...)*

"There is something strange and unusual about you. You are not *normal*."

"Not *normal*?"

"No. No. I didn't mean it *that* way, ... a *good* way."

"Then what did you mean by *that*?"

"It means that it is rare ... *very* rare that we encounter this ... someone like *you*."

"I am afraid I don't understand. I came to you to find out about my *dreams*."

"Please shuffle the tarot cards."

"Now what?"

"Cut the deck in two."

"Yes. Ok."

"Pass me the top card."

"Ok."

"This is *highly unusual*."

"What do you see?"

"I am going to ask you to let me see your hand … your palm."

"Ok … and … ?"

"I need to talk to someone. I will be right back."

"I can't wait. I have to go."

"No, please. This could be important. It *is* important!"

"I will come back at another time."

(later, talking with Kathie …)

"So *that's* what happened?"

"Yes. No answers from the Gypsies."

"Why did you not wait, Ana?"

"I was not comfortable. The whole thing was *not* comfortable."

"You should have waited for answers."

"Ok. I will go back, Kathie."

(Ana returns to the Gypsies ...)

"Yes. Yes. You come back. You sit. Be comfortable. I go fetch Gramma."

"Take your time. I am doing just fine."

"Well, Young Lady, you are just as pretty as they described you to me."

"I was advised that I should come back for more *whatever* this is."

"Yes. Yes. You surely should, but let's begin by letting *me* see what *they* saw."

"May I ask what it is that *they* saw?"

"Well, let me see."

"Ha. Ha. A lot of *seesaw* here. ... *That's funny*."

"Young Lady, you be serious. No funny stuff. Very serious going on."

"Yes, Ma'am. I will be good."

"Ok. Now you be still. I go to inner place with myself. You close eyes … *I close eyes.*"

"You want me to keep my eyes closed, right?"

"Yes. Yes. *Close eyes. Be still.*"

"Ok. I will be still."

"What I see very unusual … very ….. You are dreaming, … *remembering*, … correct?"

"Yes. Yes. You are correct."

"Very traumatic, … correct?"

"Yes. Yes. *Please* go on."

"You are special person, … correct.

"I don't know how to answer that."

"No answer. *Just statement.*"

"What can you tell me. ..... Why?"

"You have a destiny ... *very special* destiny with future."

"Can you please be more ..... Can you tell me more??"

"Not now. You come back tomorrow. I must confer with *Wise One*."

"Who is *Wise One*?"

"No questions. Come tomorrow."

(later that day, Kathie asks questions ...)

"So talk, Ana. How did it go?"

"Nothing. Nothing important, ... except maybe *she* somehow thinks I am important."

"Do you need another bopping!"

"Kathie, with all the *bopping* you want to give, I should have *calluses* by now."

"Or maybe I could knock some sense into you, Ana. ... *Come on, Ana, ... be serious.*"

"Ok. Ok. It was nothing, really. She needs to confer with the *Wise One*."

"The Wise One … the *Wise One*?? How crazy is this getting to be, Ana."

"They probably need more clients and build up drama here on purpose, don't you think, Kathie?"

"I don't know *what* to think, Ana."

"Neither do I, Kathie. Neither do I."

PLANNING

"Ana, are you ok? You have been sitting there for hours doing nothing."

"Oh, I am doing something all right. I am planning how to find my sister, Kathie."

"Which one? ... *Past* life ... or *this* life?"

"I know you're joking, ... but this is serious to me."

"No. I am *not* joking, Ana. That was a serious question."

"I am thinking about the sister Jonathan thought was me."

"You're talking about the New York girl, *right*?"

"Yes, ... and something tells me that she needs me, Kathie."

"So, are you becoming *psychic*, or something like that, Ana?"

"It's just a feeling ... a very strange, *strong* feeling."

"Don't you think you already have too much on your plate?"

"This is a real flesh and blood sister; … no question about if she's *real* or not."

"I am not questioning your concerns, but … whether you're *up* for all this, Ana."

"Well, we will see. I have decided. … I am going to New York."

"Ana, Ana, Ana, … what am I going to do with you?"

"Just be my friend, my *best* friend, … and … go along with my whims, Kathie."

"These adventures of yours are *way* more than *whims*. Don't you think you need a plan here or something?"

"That is what I have been doing, … coming up with a plan."

"Ok. Let's hear your plan."

"Kathie, it includes *you*."

"*Me*? … NO. Wait a minute. I have to think about anything you might come up with here."

"Look what *you* got me into with that *being a spokesperson* bit for UTOPIA, Kathie."

"Yes, but it worked out well, didn't it?"

"Yes, and my plan will work out for the good, too."

"Ok. Let's hear your plan, Ana."

"Well, … I don't have it all completely figured out yet, … *but* … it's a really good plan."

"Ana, you are so good at *mumbo jumbo* talk."

"Well, I will tell you all the details tomorrow, after I work them all out. Ok?"

"Ok, Ana. Ok."

(The next day …)

"Ok, Kathie. Do you want to hear our plan?"

"Ok, Ana. Let's hear … *'OUR'* … plan."

"We go to New York. We go to the restaurant and wait for her to show up."

"And … ?"

"That's it. Pretty easy, huh?"

"Ana, I can see *'YOU'* have put some thought into … *'YOUR PLAN'*, … haven't you."

"I wasn't just sitting there all day yesterday doing *nothing*."

"Really!? *That's* not a well thought out plan, Ana. Just go to the restaurant and wait for her to show up?? … Ana, let's think this through some more. … Isn't your twin sister your *look alike sister*?"

"Yes. Jonathan thought she was *me*."

"So, … don't you think everyone at that restaurant that knows *her* will think that … *YOU* … are *her*?"

"I never thought about that, Kathie."

"I am sure there is *more* about this venture that you haven't thought thru."

"Kathie, you're right. I *am* tired, … brain-dead, … *and* confused."

"Now *that* is rational thinking. Why don't you let *me* come up with a plan."

"Now, Kathie, *that* is a good plan."

(Later that evening …)

"Ok, Kathie, my *wise* and *know what's best* friend, … what kind of plan have you come up with?"

"A thought out, … practical, … feasible plan that makes sense."

"Ok. Ok. Good going. Let's hear it. What is *your* plan?"

"We stay home and recuperate."

"Kathie, I am serious. *Very* serious about this."

"So am I, Ana. You could be running right into serious trouble going half-cocked like this."

"So that kind of makes sense, I guess."

"I *do* have some thoughts about how to approach this *wisely*."

"I'm listening, Kathie. I'm listening."

"Ok. Listen to this idea and see what you think."

"I'm listening."

"You contact your *special* agency and have *them* do the *dirty work*."

"*Dirty work?*"

"That's just an expression that says *they* deal with any dangers or problems, Ana."

"*Dangers*? What kind of *dangers*?"

"Ana, that's what we *don't* want to know. Let *them* investigate. That's what the FBI and CIA people do best."

"See, … now *that* is a good plan. I *knew* you would come up with a good plan."

"Ok, Ana, … make your contacts."

"I'll get right on it, Kathie."

(A week goes by …)

"Kathie. Kathie. They found her."

"That was fast, Ana. It was only last week you hired them."

"They know that I never quibble about the bill. That's why we get good service."

"Well, let's hear it. Details. Details, Ana. Come on."

"She moves around, and the initial reports say she may be in some sort of trouble."

"See. See, Ana, it's a good thing we *didn't* follow up on *your* plan to go to New York *blindfolded*, so to speak."

"Yes, Kathie. You were *right* this time. This report is *very* kind of scary. Look at this statement … DANGER!"

"Read some more. … What else does it say?"

"It says this is *preliminary* … a *first* report, … but I should be aware of *DANGER*."

"What do you think we should do, Ana?"

"They're requesting to get *really* involved, and they need my ok to do so."

"Give it, Ana. Give it. It sure was the right thing to turn this over to them, wasn't it?"

"Yes, Kathie. That was a good call on *your* part. I will give my consent for full participation on *their* part."

"Sic 'em, Ana. Sic 'em!"

(a couple days later …)

"Kathie, the reports are coming in, one report a day; and it's not sounding good for my sister."

"Details, Ana. Details."

"Well, … she is involved with some *bad* people … *mafia* people … DANGEROUS people."

"*How* is she involved?"

"She is a witness to some very serious crimes, Kathie."

"Was she part of it? … Involved in some way?"

"The report doesn't say. Just that she is in *deep trouble* …and … in *danger*."

"What should we do, Ana?"

"I don't know. We will have to receive more reports. We get one a day."

"How many reports so far?"

"This will be the seventh, … and they get more ominous every time."

"What to do. ... What to do, Ana?"

(Days go by ... reports continue ...)

"Ana, this is serious."

"I know, Kathie. I have read all the reports, too."

"These are *bad* people. ... Can the agency do something *more* than *investigate*?"

"I will see. I will ask."

(Later, ... the reply ...)

"What was the answer, Ana?"

"The answer was a question, Kathie."

"And...?"

"And they want to know how *far* I am willing to ask them to go."

"What does *that* mean, Ana?"

"I have a good idea they are asking if ... they have *permission* to *eliminate* the problem."

"*Eliminate the problem*? ... Does *that* mean what I *think* it means? ... Well, I'm not sure we want to go there ... at least not yet."

"No. No. We *never* want to go there, Kathie. ... *Never*."

"*Good* girl, Ana. I agree."

NEW REPORT

"Ana, did you read the new report?"

"Yes, I did, ... and it's heartbreaking."

"She was in the trauma ward for two weeks."

"Kathie, she could have *died*, and I would *never* have had the chance to meet my sister."

"Well, she *cannot* ... *should not* have to sustain *any more* broken bones."

"She is living a *horrible* existence."

"Well, we should let the agency *do* what they *do*."

"You *do* know what they're capable of, don't you, Ana?"

"Yes, but I can't condone that kind of retribution."

"Did you look at those pictures taken at the hospital?"

"I actually spent last night looking, ... thinking, ... imagining, ... and crying, Kathie."

"Ana, let me be in charge of reviewing the reports. ... Those pictures are *far too graphic* for anybody to see."

"Yes, Kathie. My emotions are going wild ... anger, ... hurt, ... sad, ... revenge ..."

"Well, we need to keep our emotions in check ... right?"

"*That* is hard, ... *very* hard after reviewing all this, Kathie."

"But we *must*. If we don't, we could be putting your sister in more danger, Ana."

"I just realized we don't even know her name."

"Wow. *That* should be priority number one."

"Yes. Yes. And then ...???"

"Yes, Ana ... and then ...we'll do what we have to do."

(Ana talks to her special agency ...)

"Ok. They're on board. I gave them the *go ahead*, ... *except* for the *ELIMINATION* thing."

"Well, I am anxious to see what plan *they* come up with, Ana."

"They are all ex CIA, FBI, or Interpol people, Kathie. I should think they are capable of coming up with *something*."

"I would like to know what *something* is."

"They have my *go ahead*. We are going to find out, aren't we?"

(Later ...)

"Ana, I just received a notice saying to be *prepared*."

"*Prepared* for what, Kathie?"

"Well, whatever it is, I am sure we WON'T be *prepared*."

"Look. They're asking for us to give them a picture ... a current facial picture of *you*, Ana."

"Since my twin sister resembles *me*, … I think that is needed by them to identify *her*."

"Well, I hope they succeed, … and as *soon* as possible, Ana."

"And as *safe* as possible, Kathie."

THE HAPPENING

"Ana! Ana! You have been contacted, and it says URGENT-- REQUEST IMMEDIATE REPLY. … What do you think is happening?"

"I *have* a secret phone number, … but I am *only* supposed to use it in *emergencies*."

"Well, Ana, don't you think URGENT is classified as an *emergency*!?"

"Ok. Yes, but I have to confirm that I am *alone*; … only *one* person is privileged to listen, Kathie."

"Ok. I understand. Just go make your secret call, Ana."

(Minutes later …)

"Kathy, … it's *ON*."

"What's *ON*, Ana??"

"She is in danger of being *eliminated*. ... That's the term they used."

"You're talking about what your agency just told you?"

"Yes."

"And so whatever is going to happen, ... they need to do *fast*!"

"I gave them permission to *ACT*."

"*To ACT*? ... What does *that* mean, Ana?"

"We're going to kidnap her, Kathie."

"Are you kidding?"

"It is *their* idea, ... *their* solution. She won't even *know* she is being taken to *safety*."

"So ... all of this is going to be a *surprise* to your sister?"

"Yes. She won't be *in* on it until she arrives here. ... Isn't that *exciting*!?"

"Wow. I don't know what to *say* ... or what to *think*, Ana."

"Kathie, I already *gave* the go ahead … *it's happening*."

"Wow. And wow, again. We have to think this through."

"Kathie, I think we just possibly saved my sister's life."

"We don't even *know* your sister's *name*, … and she is being kidnapped for *her* own good, … and brought here to us….."

"Yes. Yes. It's for her own good, … *don't you agree?*"

"Yes. Yes, Ana. I *guess* so, … but … we have to anticipate *her* reaction to all of this."

"Yes, Kathie, you're right. We *better* come up with a plan should the agency be able to pull this kidnapping off. ….. It's *saving* her, … *we're* saving her; … *she* will understand."

"Ana, that all *sounds* good, … but … put yourself in *her* shoes. *She* is going to be *traumatized* big time."

"Yes, you're right, Kathie. We have to think this through, … and … be *ready* to explain all this to *her*."

(Two days later …)

"Ana, we just received another urgent message ... *they HAVE HER.*"

"That's *great* news. ... She is *safe*. ... Does it say *how* she is doing, Kathie?"

"Apparently, she is *drugged out* and *unconscious*, ... and ... they're waiting for further instructions from *you*."

"I will make contact and tell them to bring her *here*. ….. Yes. Yes, ... and as *soon* as possible; ... by plane ... or however is the *fastest* way to get her here."

"We need to *prepare* for this event. ... *And* ... you should call Dr. Mesmer, ... since he *is* the *father* to *both* of you, Ana."

"Yes. Yes, Kathie. I will call him right away."

(A short time later ...)

"Kathie, I called ... and he sounds *excited*. ... He will be here as *soon* as we call him. …..
Wow, Kathie. Can you believe this is really happening?"

"Well, yes. ... This is a *big deal* alright, ... and *we* better get planning how *we're* going to handle this, Ana. …..
We're going to need your *father's* expertise on how to

handle the drama that your *new found, no-named sister* is about to experience."

"She is my *blood* sister. ... She will handle this just as I would, Kathie."

And ...?

"And you're *right*. ... *This* is going to be *traumatic*. ... I'll call Dr. Mesmer *today*."

"*Great* idea. ... And, ... Ana, ... I have a plan ... a *good* plan."

"I'm listening, Kathie."

"We have *two days* to get that back bedroom made up like a *hospital* room; ... and when she arrives, ... she will be *unconscious*, as your special agency said she would be. ... When your sister wakes up, she will *think* she is in a *hospital*. ... We could have Dr. Mesmer be her attending doctor."

"Wow, Kathie. *That* might just work."

"Hurry, Ana. Go hire a *real* nurse to sit with her until she wakes up. I will start preparing a hospital-looking room."

"That is the *best plan ever*, Kathie. After that, we will just play *it by ear*."

PLAN WORKS

"They're bringing her now. How did you get that ambulance, Ana?"

"Money, Kathie, ... money. ... Shh ... shh ... Don't wake her. Show them where to take her, ... get the nurse ready, ... and I'll call my father."

"Ana, this is working out perfectly, ... so far."

"Don't be so jubilant *yet*. The *true test* is going to be when my sister wakes up."

"*So good so far.*"

"Yes, Ana. ... *So FAR so good.*"

THE NEIGHBORS SAW

"Ana, … you're *already* in trouble. … You will have a *lot* of explaining to do."

"What are you talking about, Kathie?"

"Our neighbors saw the ambulance pull up and went to investigate."

"So …?"

"*So*, … they saw *you* all thin, … emaciated, … looking terrible, Ana."

"But that *wasn't* me.

"*They* don't know about your look-alike twin sister, … and we can't let *anybody* know about her. … We don't need bad people coming here looking for her."

"You're right, Kathie. *She* will have to be *our* secret."

"*That* will be hard to do, Ana. I saw our neighbor take a picture with her phone when they were wheeling *you* in."

"She is such a gossip. Everyone will see those pictures of *my* bruised face and short hair."

"Yes, you're somehow going to have to *grow long hair* and *heal up that black eye and bruises* … and *fast*, Ana."

"My twin sister looks pretty bad, doesn't she? … We will *give* … and *get* her … the best care ever, won't we, Kathie."

"Yes, *anything* for my *two* best friends in the world."

"What would I do, … no … what would *we* do … without you, Kathie?"

"Well, you both *do* have me, … and I hope *she* takes to me as well as *you* do."

"She will. … If she is anything like me, *she will*."

THE ENCOUNTER

"Ana, It's been *two* days and she is *still* not waking up."

"Well, Dr. Mesmer has been looking in on her twice a day; and he has his medical doctor friend visiting her every couple of hours. My sister is in very good hands."

"Have they explained why she is *not* waking up?"

"Yes. They think my CIA guys must have used really powerful drugs to get away with kidnapping her as they did, Kathie."

"Well, looking at her in that emaciated state she is in, I hope they didn't hurt her."

"We can do nothing but be grateful that they accomplished their mission; … and … we will take over from here on out, Kathie."

"Ana, we have to think how to handle all this when she finally … and *fully* awakens."

"How do you think she will react when she sees *me* for the first time?"

"Ana, you need to stop peeking in the door to look at her. Can you imagine what she will go through if she sees *herself* at the door?"

"Yes. *That* could be *shocking*. Ha. Ha."

"Ana, *that* could be *serious*. We have to be *delicate* about this."

"A lot of drama here, Kathie."

"Yes, but it is all *good* drama. We are no longer a *twosome*, … but … a *threesome*."

"Yes, Kathie, … a *threesome*."

WHO ARE YOU?

"How are you feeling, Young Lady?"

"I hurt. ... Who are *you*?"

"I am Doctor Mesmer."

"*Where* am I?"

"You are being very well cared for right here. ... This is Nurse Sarah Perkins. She will be your constant companion until you are better."

"Am I *in custody* ... *protective custody*, as the detectives said I would be?"

"Yes. You are in *protective custody*."

"You know *they* have ways of finding me."

"How do you *mean* that?"

"I am scared ... and I have *reason* to be. ... As I explained to the other detectives, they have their people infiltrated in the police bureau; ... and ... I don't trust *anyone*."

"Well, you are *far away* from the bad people, … and … I assure you, Young Lady, that you are in a *very* secure place."

"Well, you promised me *protection*."

"Yes, and I said you're *safe* here, … and all *you* need to think about is healing up your wounds."

"Yes, they did a job on me, alright. … I thought I was *done for*."

"You were drugged up pretty bad … and … now I advise that you concentrate on resting and recuperation."

"Yes, I *am* groggy … and *very* tired. I need to *sleep*."

(Later …)

"Well, Dr. Mesmer, … what are your thoughts?"

"Whoever did this to her should be severely ….."

"Is she ok? … How do you think she is reacting to all this?"

"I believe she *thinks* she is in *protective custody* … *out of danger*. … And she seems to accept that."

"Well, Doctor, *that* is a relief. What should we do now?"

"Nothing more than you have been doing. … She is going to need some extensive therapy, and I am totally on board for that. … I advise that she find out the truth *very* slowly."

"I understand, Dr. Mesmer. … *Slow and easy.*"

BACK BEDROOM

"Nurse Perkins, … please wake up."

"Yes. Yes. I am awake now. I apologize for falling asleep. What can I do for you, Honey?"

"Do you know about this place?"

"What is it you want to know?"

"Is it *haunted*?"

"Why would you ask that?"

"*Because* … I saw a *ghost!*"

"You saw *what*?"

"At the door … I saw *myself* … peeking in … and *looking at me*."

"You saw *yourself* peeking in … and looking at you?"

"Yes. Yes. *That's* what I am saying, Nurse Perkins."

"Well, … let me go investigate. I will be right back."

(In the other room …)

"Listen, Ms. Romanov, … she *saw* you. How do I explain *that* to her?"

"*OH.* … I am *so* sorry. … I just wanted to be sure she is ok."

"Well, … what do I tell her?"

"Just tell her that she probably is just *still* under the influence of all those drugs she was given."

"Well ok, … I will try, … but … I don't think she is going to buy that story."

(Later …)

"Dr. Mesmer, I think I might have *goofed* … *blown it*."

"So … she *saw* you, Ana?"

"How did *you* know? … Are you becoming *psychic*?"

"No. It's a little more simple than that. … I am in regular communication with your nurse on duty, and she informed me of your *faux pas*."

"So … you're keeping good tabs on my sister?"

"No, … I am keeping *very good* tabs on *both* of my daughters. I am as worried about *you* as I am her, Ana."

"I am ok. … I am just a little bit *excited* about all of this."

"And *that* very much concerns me. We have to reveal *the truth* to our new found relative, … and … *the sooner, the better*."

"And *how* are we going to accomplish *that, Father*?"

"*Delicately*, of course. And we're *all* going to have to embrace the fact that we are *family* here."

"*Family. Family.* I like that. Are you up for that, *Father*?"

"I will if you will, *Daughter*."

(Dr. Mesmer asks for an update …)

"Nurse Perkins, I need your report. How is she doing?"

"I think I have information that is of value to you, Doctor."

"And what might that be?"

"Remember my asking what my new patient's name is?"

"Yes, … and we explained to you that we didn't know her name."

"Well, Doctor, … you do *now*. … Her name is *Maria*."

"Well, I am going to see that you get a raise to your salary for your quick thinking."

"And, Doctor, I should also mention that she doesn't have a *last* name."

"Are you sure about that? *Everybody* has a last name."

"We have been having deep conversations to keep from being bored, … and … there is much more that you might be interested in knowing."

"I can see that the raise you're getting is going to be quite sizable, Nurse Perkins."

"Well, Dr. Mesmer, I am definitely inspired by that; … and you, Sir, can look forward to a whole lot more valuable information."

"Good work, Nurse. … *Great* work."

(Dr. Mesmer talks with Ana a little later …)

"I need to inform you that we have a *very* valuable asset in the form of Nurse Perkins."

"She came highly recommended, … but what inspired *that* little speech?"

"She is engaging with our patient Maria on a scale that would be *hard* to duplicate."

"In other words, Doctor, she is *doing a good job*."

"Yes, if you want to put it *simply*. … Yes."

"Well, she found out Maria's first name, … and she found out there was *nothing* to find on a *last* name."

"I couldn't have put it more eloquently myself."

"And we will be very generous with her new salary."

"That is very advisable."

"Well, when do we …..?"

"Be patient. This is very important. I will advise when the time is appropriate, … *Daughter*."

"Patience is *not* my virtue, … but I will abide by your directives, … *Father*."

STORYTELLING

"Boy ... has she been telling me *quite* the stories. She has lived a *sordid life*, Dr. Mesmer."

"I assumed that from what we have already learned; ... and you, Nurse Perkins, are providing me with *valuable* information that will *greatly* enhance her recovery."

"I am very much enjoying my participation in her recovery. This has been my most rewarding endeavor in a long time."

"Well, I am anxious to hear your retelling of her stories. *That* will greatly benefit what we're trying to do here; ... and we are so thankful we found you, Nurse."

"Well, the stories are graphic ... *and* ... traumatic, and Maria has had no qualms about providing details. ... She has endured *a lot*."

"I am sure you know this is to remain confidential, Nurse Perkins."

"Yes, Dr. Mesmer. I assumed that."

"I will want to tape record your retelling of Maria's story."

"Doctor, she is very cooperative and seems to be anxious to tell … *her* story."

"Do you think she would be agreeable to an *open* tape recording from here on out?"

"Well, Dr. Mesmer, I will work on seeing about that first thing tomorrow."

(The next morning …)

"Good morning, Maria. I haven't visited with you lately, and I miss getting to know you better."

"Well, Dr. Mesmer, you seem to be a very nice, handsome man; … and I have heard some *very* nice things about you."

"Well then, … we're off to a great start, aren't we."

"Nurse Perkins tells me you are a *special* kind of doctor … a therapist, … psychiatrist, … and counselor."

"Yes,… and maybe a little *more* than that, … when it comes to *you*."

"Well, … that sounds kind of intriguing, Doctor."

"Maria, … *you* are special, … *very* special to a lot of people."

"Yes, … I know *they* want me to be … *eliminated*, … as they put it."

"No. … *That* is in your past. … If you want, your *whole future* can be different … *very different*."

"You're going to make me cry, Doctor. … I haven't had the best life."

"It's ok to cry a little, Maria. You go ahead. … I will leave now, … but I will be back with some very important people I want you to meet."

"Oh, Doctor, you give me hope. … You don't know how much that means to me."

"Well, Young Lady, your life is about to change … *drastically*."

"Thank you … thank you … *thank you*, Dr. Mesmer."

"You be anticipating good things. … I will bring your new friends with me … and maybe some *shocking surprises*."

"*Shocking surprises*? … I hope you mean that in a *good* way, Doctor."

"In a *very* good way, … the *best* of way for you, Young Lady."

"Wow. … I will try to look my best. … I can't wait."

REVELATION

"Well good morning, Maria. How are you feeling?"

"Well, my legs are feeling better. I would like to get out of bed, Nurse."

"Well, we will just see about that; ... but we don't want to rush into anything without doctor's approval."

"Is *this* the day?"

"That is what I've been told. ... Are you excited?"

"*Scared*. ... I am a little scared. ... I don't know what to expect."

"Well, I don't want to over dramatize, ... but this *is* an important day for you."

"What should I expect?"

"Well, ... I *do* know that I am excited for you, Maria."

"Can you help me be presentable? ... I used to be pretty."

"Yes, … I have brought you some make up; … and you still *are very* pretty."

"What time am I supposed to meet those people?"

"You have time to be presentable. I think sometime this afternoon."

"How should I act?"

"You should be prepared for, … I don't know how to put this, … some rather *stunning* revelations."

"You're scaring me, Nurse Perkins."

"Oh no. Oh no. I am just trying to *prepare* you. … Don't be scared. It's all good."

"Wow. Wow. I don't know if I am *ready* to make new friends."

"These are more than friends, … more like *family*."

"*Family*? … I don't have family. … I am an orphan."

"I have said too much. … Calm down. … It will all be good, Maria."

"Now, … I *am* nervous."

"You just calm down. I will have Dr. Mesmer come in and talk with you. ... Would that be alright?"

"Yes. Please do that. I like him. I trust him. I *want* to speak to him."

"I will go see if he has arrived. ... Just you remain calm now."

(Nurse Perkins steps out of the room to talk with Dr. Mesmer ...)

"Dr. Mesmer, ... thank goodness you're here. I might have said too much."

"Calm down, Nurse. ... Everything will be alright."

"She wants to see you, ... talk to you. ... I might have upset her."

"How? ... What did you say?"

"I don't know. Maybe something about *family*. ... I don't remember exactly."

"It's ok. It's all ok, Nurse Perkins. She will have to know everything, ... and it's a good head start. You might have done a *good* thing, actually."

"Thank you, Doctor. Thank you. I was worried I said too much."

"You just go home for now and relax. I will take over from here."

"Thank you, Doctor. Thank you."

(Dr. Mesmer enters Maria's room …)

"Well … well, … can I ask how you're feeling, Maria?"

"I am glad I can talk to you *before* I meet all those people."

"Well, I might have misled you. … There are *not* a *lot* of people that I want you to meet."

"Oh. I misunderstood. … I feel better already. … *How many*?"

"Just two, … one other person … and myself."

"Just two of you? … That's not so bad. … Now I am *not* so nervous, Dr. Mesmer."

"Good. Very good, … but … I must tell you something."

"Ok. Ok. *What* must you tell me?"

"Well, let's just say, … I *hope* you will feel, as we do, … that *what* we have to tell you … is *wonderful*."

"*Wonderful*, Doctor? … My life has been anything *but* … wonderful."

"Well, I hope *this* day … *that* all changes for you, Maria."

"*That* would be wonderful, Dr. Mesmer."

(A short time later …)

"Well, Maria, … before I introduce you, I want to give you a little background, … a little history of what we have discovered."

"Who is *we*?"

"You will find out soon enough, … but it's important for you to know this."

"Dr. Mesmer, you're being suspenseful. … This is becoming fun."

"Yes, … this *is* fun … and also *wonderful*."

"I am listening to your story, Dr. Mesmer."

"Yes. This is a story, … a good story … that has been in the making for some time now."

"What's the story about?"

"It's about a wonderful girl who found out that she had *a twin sister* she did not know about."

"So, the story is about a girl that discovered she had a *twin sister*, and … she didn't know that, Dr. Mesmer?"

"Yes. … And it's quite a story, Maria."

"That *is* an interesting story, Dr. Mesmer."

"And there is more, Maria."

"I'm listening, Dr. Mesmer."

"They didn't know who their *father* was either."

"I can relate to *that* story, Dr. Mesmer. … It could have been … *my story* … somewhat."

"Do you need a handkerchief, Maria?"

"Yes, Doctor. I'm sorry for tearing up. That story kind of hits home."

"Well, Maria, ... are you ready for the ... *kicker*?"

"I'll stop crying here, Doctor. ... What is the ... *kicker*?"

"That is *YOU* and your *TWIN SISTER'S* story."

"What!? ... What!? ... I guess I'll *not* stop crying right now."

"And ... there is even more to come ..."

"I'm sorry, Dr. Mesmer, ... I am starting to bawl here."

*(D r. Mesmer motions for Ana
to enter the room ...)*

"Maria, may I introduce you to your sister, ... your *TWIN SISTER*."

"Hi Maria. ... I am your sister, Anastacia."

"Wow. ... Hi Anastacia. ... You look like me, ... only prettier. ... I have to stop crying here. ... I am so happy. ... Can I have a *hug*?"

"How about a *threesome*? ... *Our* father ... and my new found sister. ... All in a great big hug! ... Come here, Dr. Mesmer, ... *Father*."

IT IS A *GOOD* MORNING

(Ana knocks on Maria's door …)

"Good morning, Maria. … May I come in?"

"Yes. … Sure. ….. You're very pretty."

"Well, I just put makeup on … I'm *not* so pretty without *lots* of makeup on."

"I *used* to be pretty … once … too."

"Well, … *you're* going to be as pretty as I am … once I share all my makeup with *you.*"

"That will be really nice. … You *do* kind of look like me … or … I look like *you* … or something like that."

"Maria, … we are *twin sisters* … through and through; and, … *Sis*, … we have a *lot* of catching up to do."

"You're nice. … I like that."

"Maria, you don't know how long I have waited for this day. … Excuse me a little. … I don't mean to cry."

"Ana, … can I call you *Ana*? … This makes me *so* happy. … I am crying right along with you."

"Well, we both better stop crying here. … *We* have better things to do. … How are your legs? … Do you think you can walk?"

"I can try … if you will help me."

"Ok. Let's try. … I have a lot to show you."

(Ana helps Maria try to walk …)

"How is this, Maria? … What do you think? ….. Hum. … A little wobbly. … I think we should start off in that wheelchair we brought you."

"Yes. I think I am going to need to go slowly. … They did a job on me."

"Yes, … well *that* is in the *far past*. … You won't have to worry about *anything* like that *ever again*. … *You're very safe here*."

"Ana, … where am I?"

"There is a lot to tell you; … and if you want, *you*, my sister, are *HOME*."

"I have never had a *home*. ... Did I tell you, ... I am an *orphan*?"

"No, ... but I bet you have an interesting story to tell."

"Yes, ... I probably do; ... and I never *knew* ... or ever ever *thought* I had a sister ... or a *twin* sister. That is quite a shock to me."

"Yes, I can imagine, Maria. ... We were worried how you would take all this."

"To tell the truth, I *am* in shock. ... I still can't believe all this. ... Are you sure I'm not *dreaming,* Ana?"

"If you *are* ... this is going to be the *best dream ever, Sis.*"

"*Sis ... Sister ...* am I *really* your sister?"

"You better believe it, ... and I can't wait to show you around. ... And my best friend is dying to meet you. ... May I bring her in?"

"Do I look presentable?"

"Maria, you look wonderful. ... I want to introduce you to the best friend anyone could ever have ... *Kathie*!... Come on in!"

(Kathie enters …)

"Hi Maria. … I'm Kathie. … I am so *glad* to finally meet you."

"I am glad to meet you too, Kathie."

"So, … can we get you into that wheelchair and show you around?"

"Sure, Ana, … if you want to."

"Boy, … do we *ever* want to. … Are you ready?"

"I'm ready."

(The girls wheel Maria out of her room …)

"Wow. … This is *big*. … This is *beautiful*. … Is this a *house*?"

"This, Maria, is a *complex*."

"This is a *complex*? … I don't know what that means, Kathie."

"This is a pretty big place. … It is a lot of very nice, shall we say, … *homes*."

"If you don't mind me asking, … how can you pay for all this, Ana?"

"Well, I was going to get around to telling you … at some point, … so … why not now."

"*Why not now*, … what does *tha*t mean?"

"Our mother left us a sizable inheritance, Maria."

"I don't understand. … What does *that* mean?"

"*That* means you don't have to ever again *worry* about your next *meal*."

"*That* sounds like you're trying to be funny, Sister."

"Yes, … a little … but I hope you will get used to my humor."

"Well, I like you already … *a lot* … BOTH of you; … and I can see you want to be my friends. … I *need* friends. … *Boy, do I need friends*."

"Well, Maria, … we are on board to be *way* more than just your *friends*. … Are you ok with that?"

"Yes, … I am ok with that."

SECTION NINE

HAPPY FAMILY

HAPPY FAMILY

"Good morning, Kathie. I hope I didn't startle you."

"Oh, Maria, … I didn't know you were up yet. … How did you sleep? … Last night you seemed a little restless."

"I apologize. … I am *that* way all the time. … I have always had to be on guard most of my life."

"Well, I understand you're going to do *therapy sessions* with Dr. Mesmer, your *father*. *That* will help you adjust."

"*Father* … *father*. … I have to get used to that. I never in my *wildest dreams* ever thought my life would come to this, Kathie."

"Well, I am sure it will take some time to adjust, Maria."

"Kathie, … you … and Anastacia have been so nice to me."

"Maria, you don't know how hard your sister looked to find you … *and* your shared father."

"What are you saying? … She didn't always know him? … *Our father*?"

"Heavens no. … He didn't even *know* he had two daughters … until recently."

"*Wow*. … I have a lot to catch up on, don't I?"

"Girl, you sure do … *and* … it's all good."

"Boy oh boy, … you guys sure are changing my outlook on life, Kathie."

"Well, … I hope you like it, Maria."

"Are you kidding? … I have to pinch myself every five minutes to see if I'm *dreaming*."

"Boy, … I can see you are very much like your *sister*."

"I hope so. … I really really like her."

"So, … Kathie, … where *is* Ana?"

"She is outside in the garden … *studying*."

"*Studying*? … What is she studying?"

"She is trying to help her boyfriend by studying. ….. It's a long story. … Why don't you join her in the garden area, … and I will bring some drinks and join you."

"Are you sure I won't be disturbing her studies?"

"It's really not studying. … We're taking some very unusual classes, and she wants to be prepared. … I am sure she would like to share about her classes with you."

"If you're sure it's ok … I would like to be a part of whatever you guys are doing, Kathie."

"Why don't you go see, Maria. … I will join you with some cold drinks."

(Maria goes to the garden …)

"Excuse me, Ana, … Kathie said you wouldn't mind if I join you. … This is very beautiful out here. … Look at all these flowers."

"This is the best place to be in the morning, … and … this is the perfect place for us to get to know each other, Maria."

"Well, this is the prettiest garden I have ever seen. … We have *nothing* like this where I come from."

"Well, I might have gone a little overboard with the flowers."

"Oh no. ... This is perfect ... *wonderful*.... This is like some kind of paradise."

"Maria, I am so glad you like this place."

"Ana, I feel like I am in some kind of special dream; ... and ... if I am, ... I don't *ever* want to wake up."

"Well, Maria, ... this is *real* ... as *real* as it can get."

"*Oh.* ... I'm sorry. ... I am going to cry."

"Ok, Maria, ... come here. ... It's time for another hug. ... Ok?"

"I am becoming happy, ... *so happy.* ... I really don't know what to say."

"You have *said* all I want to hear with those tears. ..... We're going to have to get some more tissues, aren't we?"

"This is the *best cry* I have ever had, Ana."

"Me too. ... *Me too.*"

(Later, Ana and Kathie talk ...)

"That was the *best* afternoon ever. ... We talked and talked."

"Ana, that's why I left after I brought your drinks."

"Kathie, I knew what you were doing. ... I needed time *alone* with her, ... and I told her about the classes we're taking with Dr. Phenom and his colleagues."

"Well, you *are* bonding with her *fast*. ... I hope I don't have a reason to be *jealous*."

"Kathie, you will *always* be at the top of my list."

"Ana, did you forget about *Tatiana*?"

"Tatiana was in my *last* life ... *if* my past life regressions are real."

"Should we take Maria to our class Friday to see what she thinks about all this, Ana?"

"Yes. Definitely. ... She needs to know about *everything* we are up to ... if we want to *truly* bond with her."

(Later that day ...)

"Kathie, ... I spoke with Maria, ... and ... she is *very* much open to *anything* we are involved in."

"Great, Ana. ... We'll take her to our past life regression class on Friday."

FRIDAY IN REGRESSION CLASS

"Well, ... what happens now, Kathie?"

"Your sister has already volunteered *last* week, Maria."

"If Ana has experienced this, ... I want to do it also, Kathie."

"Are you *sure*, Maria?"

"Yes. ... Look, ... they are doing *multiple* regressions at the same time."

"Let's *both* do it. ... Volunteer to do it *together* at the same time, Kathie."

"Ok. ... But it may not work for me. ... I am known as the *skeptical* one."

(after the regression session with Maria and Kathie, Ana wants information ...)

"Maria, ... what is this about *Kathie*?"

"She was in that regression session, … and … apparently she was a *very* good candidate."

"*Were* you with her?"

"Yes, Ana, … and she went very deep into some *very dramatic* past life memories."

"Wow, Maria. … Kathie has always been so *skeptical*."

"Yes. … And they had to bring her up *fast*! … She was *terrified*, Ana."

"Did she *say* anything?"

"Yes. *Yes*. … She kept saying something about being jealous *of herself*."

"Well, I definitely need to know about *that* regression."

"Here she comes now, Ana, ….."

"Well hello, Kathie, … I hear you went under quite deep."
"I owe *you* an apology, Ana."

"I think I know … it's … about *Tatiana*, … isn't it Kathie?"

"Yes. Yes. I was there *with you* in that same memory *you* had, Ana."

"So … you … have been jealous of …*yourself*??"

"Yes! … It all makes sense now. … *I* was your sister *Tatiana* in our past life in Russia. … *I* came over here to this time with you … and … there is *much* more. ….. *Maria* was *our baby sister* in that life, Ana."

"Wow! … And *wow*, again! … It all makes perfect sense, Kathie."

"Yes. … *That* life was tragic. … Let's make this one GREAT!"

"*Three sisters reunited* … at last."

"So, … Kathie, … *you* were Tatiana in that past life with Ana in Russia?"

"Yes, Maria. … I have been jealous of *my* previous life's SELF!"

WONDERFUL NEW LIFE

"Kathie, who is that handsome man in that picture over there? … He looks familiar to me."

"Maria, you *have* met him. ... *That* is Jonathan. ... He is Anastacia's boyfriend. ... You saw him in New York."

"I *what*? ... I don't remember that."

"Jonathan said he approached you in some restaurant. He thought you were Ana, ... and ... you told him to *go away*. ... Do you remember *that* incident?"

"No. ... But I was probably trying to *avoid* him getting badly beaten up, Kathie."

"How so, Maria?"

"In my other life in New York, I was always being approached by other men, ... and ... they were then all badly beaten up."

"I sense a story here. ... Do you want to tell it?"

"He was *very* jealous ... and also a *very dangerous* man."

"I take it *he* was your *boyfriend* at the time?"

"No. ... *He* was like a *brother*. ... I was taken into what I learned was a *Mafia-like* family. ... I think they needed me for some kind of *front*. ... I witnessed a lot of *bad things*, Kathie."

"Oh. … You're starting to tear up. … We won't talk about that kind of stuff. … Let's talk about our regression session, ok …..?"

"I can't believe it, Kathie. … Do you think what I experienced are *real* past life memories?"

"Well, Maria, … I *used* to be super skeptical; … and now … I am in *awe* by all of this. … Remember, I *also* did the *past life regression*."

"What did *you* experience, Kathie?"

"I was *there*. … I remember, just as Ana did. … We were sisters back then. … I was named *Tatiana* in that life, … and … in *this* life … I was jealous *of myself*."

"Kathie, this is a little confusing to me."

"I know. … I know. … I didn't explain it correctly, … but now … I am no longer *skeptical*. … That's the point I'm trying to make here."

"Well, if all those past life memories are *real*, … I was your *true sister* back then, Kathie. … We were *all three sisters* in *that* life back in Russia."

"Yes. … *And*, … Maria, … we are *all sisters* here and now, … two by *blood* … and one by *desire*. … All three of us in this *wonderful new life*."

"Kathie, … I like the sound of that … *WONDERFUL NEW LIFE!*"

JONATHAN IS HOME

"Jonathan, … you're home! … I am so happy to see you."

"I am happy to be home. … I missed you, Ana. … *So,* … how is it going?"

"Oh, Jonathan, … I can't wait for you to meet her. She is *everything* I could have hoped for in a sister."

"Where is she now?"

"She is out shopping with Kathie. … *My* clothes don't quite fit her."

"I heard we might have to give her *extra* portions for quite some time."

"Yes. And extra layers of *makeup*. … She has been through *a lot*, Jonathan."

"I'm excited to hear what you have to tell me, Ana."

"There's *a lot* to tell. … You have been away and missed *all* the action."

"I heard that you brought in the *BIG BOYS*."

"How did you hear about *that*?"

"I had to *approve* of that action, Ana."

"Boy, … I have a lot to learn about the *society*, don't I. *Everybody* seems to know everything … *but me*."

"Well, … you are being groomed for *big things*, Ana."

"I *need* you to explain what *that* means, Jonathan."

"Yes, Ana, … we *need* to talk."

"Yes. Yes. I *need* explanations. Please. *Please*. Talk to me. Please *do*."

"Ok, Ana. Sit down. … There is *a lot* going on in the world; … and *we* have destinies, … and *we* have been *chosen*."

"*Chosen*? … *Chosen*? … What in heaven's name does *that* mean?"

"Ana, … we have never discussed *religion*, have we?"

"No, … I guess not. … *Why*? … Is that important to what is happening?"

"Yes. Yes. That *is* related to what's happening to me … and to *you*."

"I am *so confused*, Jonathan. … I really *don't* understand."

"Ana, I am on a mission. … I have been *called upon* to educate myself with all the religions of the world, … and *that* is what I have been doing … and will *continue* to do."

"Is *that* important to you, Jonathan?"

"*That* is important for the *whole world*. … All the religions *must* come together for what is prophesied to manifest in the *near future*."

"Is the lady Angela a part of this?"

"She *is* … and *will be* … a *BIG* part of all this … just as *we* are, Ana."

"What are you talking about, Jonathan?"

"In Matthew 24:6-8: '*You will hear of wars and rumors of wars. See that you are not alarmed, for this must take place, but the end is not yet. For nation will rise against nation, and kingdom against kingdom, and there will be famines and earthquakes in various places. All these are but the beginning of the birth pains.*'"

"Wow. … That *is* a powerful prophecy. … And, … Jonathan, what about your *past life regression*? … Do you have memories?"

"I would *not* be doing what I am doing, … if I didn't."

"So … I was a *princess*. … What were *you*? … *Where* were you, Jonathan?"

"My memories were of a long time ago … from B.C. to A.D. in our dating system."

"I need to research that time period, Jonathan."

"Good idea, Ana. … Start with … the … 'BLACK BOOK.' "

"Oh. … I am *beginning* to understand … I *think*."

HER PERFECT DAY

"Kathie, … I'm so excited. … *Finally*, … I get to marry the *love of my life*. … Using the clubhouse and garden at UTOPIA is the perfect setting for my little wedding today. … I only wish my father could be here, too. ….."

"I know, Ana. … I think he probably *wanted* to be here; … but … you remember he said he just *couldn't* be here. … He said something about his wife having returned to try to work things out with him; … and since she didn't want *any* children and had left Dr. Mesmer when she found out about *you*, he felt he should decline the wedding invitation. … To make *her* happy."

"I know, … but … it would make *me* so happy if he were here."

"Well, Ana, … you look *so* beautiful. … Do you have the pink roses you wanted to carry? … Are you ready to go get *hitched*?"

"Yes, Kathie. … I am so so ready to marry the *man of my dreams*. … I just wish my father could be here. … Let's go."

"Ana, look!! ... Your father *is* here ... *and* his wife! They're coming this way, Ana."

(*Dr. Mesmer and his wife approach Ana and Kathie ...*)

"Ana, I hope you don't mind if we join you on your special day, ... and I think my *wife* has something she would like to say ... right, Honey?"

"Ana, ... I'm *so sorry* if I hurt your feelings by not wanting to meet you. ... I can be *so* stubborn and bullheaded sometimes. ... I was just *scared*. I never wanted children, ... probably because I was afraid of being a bad parent. And when Franz told me about *you*, ... I just panicked. ... Can you forgive me? ... Maybe we can just start over? ... I really *would* like to get to know you. ... I never had a daughter to pamper."

"Oh, Ms. Mesmer, ... thank you! ... That would be lovely. It will be fun to get to know *you* a little better; ... and, ... *Father*, ... I'm so glad *you're* here. ... This is no longer a *speci*al day, ... It's a *perfect* day!"

"Oh ... thank you, Ana, ... *Daughter*, ... and if you'll have me, ... I would be honored to walk you down the aisle to where Jonathan is waiting."

"Dr. Mesmer, … *Dad*, … that would be wonderful. … *Simply wonderful*!!"

ANASTACIA'S DIARY

Dear Diary .....

Oh what a perfect day!! ... Our little wedding was just perfect! ..... It was small, ... but oh so wonderful! ..... My best friend in the whole wide world was there, ... my twin sister was there, ... and my new-found father. ...Best of all, I married the love of my life. ... My Jonathan. ... My handsome, ... wonderful, ... perfect Jonathan. ..... Nothing more to be said. ... It was a perfect day!,....

And oh, ... Dear Diary, ... I am also so so excited. ..... Our little baby will soon be welcomed into the world. ... We can't wait!

RELIGION?

"Kathie, I have had a talk with Jonathan."

"And what was this talk about, Ana?"

"Religion."

"You talked about *religion*?"

"Yes. *Religion*. ... And I don't know what *to think*. ... I don't even know what *I* think, Kathie. ... Do you?"

"Ana, you are so good at the *mumbo jumbo talk*. Can you make some sense here?"

"He is conflicted. ... I think he is remembering his so-called *past life*."

"Well, *my regression* was very believable to *me*. ... I changed my thoughts on that subject *fast*."

"Me too. Me too, Kathie. ... But what to make of all *this*."

"Well, we better figure this out, don't you think?"

"Yes, yes, ... I do. What do *you* believe, Kathie?"

"You know, … as close as we are, … we have never discussed *religion*, Ana."

"Well, better late than never. … So, … *is* there … or *isn't* there??"

"I think there *has* to be, … or … how did *this* all happen??"

"Well, I think *that* is what Jonathan is doing, Kathie. … He is investigating *all around the world*."

"Do you think he *knows* yet, Ana?"

"I think we should discuss this with *him*. … Do you think he would be open to that?"

"Let's ask him. … Ok. … Let's do it!"

SECTION TEN

ADVENTURE

ADVENTURE

"Ana, ... so Jonathan wants you to *join* him?"

"So it seems, Kathie. ... He is over in Nepal. He has a *new title*, ... and is excited about his new *mission*."

"What is his *new mission* ... since he resigned his position at Superior General?"

"Well, ... as Jonathan related it to me, ... his *biological* father, Dr. David Danner, ... was very understanding. ... He apparently suspected all along."

"So, ... how is Jonathan embracing that?"

"Just as I did at first. ... When the DNA test collaborated with what he suspected, ... he confronted his new-found biological father."

"So, ... how was Dr. Danner's reaction?"

"According to Jonathan, it was *very positive*, ... *very cordial*, ... with *open arms* to his new-found family."

"Well, ... that was the *very best* conclusion one could expect, wasn't it?"

"Yes, … everything's coming together very well, … don't you think, Kathie?"

"Yes, Ana, … *life is good.*"

"By the way, … Jonathan's new title is … *Emeritus Scholar of Religious Studies.* … We may be staying at Maya Devi Temple in Lumbini with Tibetan monks."

"Life is quite the adventure."

"It sure is, Kathie. … *It sure is*!!"

THE END ... OR ... THE BEGINNING?

LIFE IS STRANGE. ... WHAT IF WE'RE ... *JUST CHARACTERS IN SOME WRITER'S IMAGINATION* ...

WELL, ... IF WE *ARE*, ... WE BETTER HAVE SOME INTERESTING TALES TO TELL: ... LIKE, ... WHAT IS ANA'S EXPECTED BABY GOING TO HAVE TO DO WITH THE FUTURE?

AND ... WHAT IS THAT ... *SECRET SOCIETY* ... THING?

AND, ... DON'T FORGET ABOUT JONATHAN AND *HIS* REGRESSION SESSIONS ...

YES, ... HE IS A VERY IMPORTANT CHARACTER. ... HE IS OFF INTO THE WORLD

DOING ... *WHAT?* ... AND,... MORE IMPORTANTLY, ... *WHY??*

AND, ... MOST IMPORTANTLY, ... IS THE PSYCHIC LADY PRESENT TO UNVEIL THE PROPHECY OF THE BLACK BOOK TO THE WORLD??

YES, ... THERE IS A LOT MORE TO THIS STORY THAT I THINK NEEDS TO BE TOLD.

DON'T YOU??

www.ingramcontent.com/pod-product-compliance
Lightning Source LLC
LaVergne TN
LVHW011941060526
838201LV00061B/4176